A WOMAN'S BATTLE FOR
GRACE

CHERYL BRODERSEN

HARVEST HOUSE PUBLISHERS
EUGENE, OREGON

A Woman's Battle for Grace
Copyright © 2018 Cheryl Brodersen
Published by Harvest House Publishers
Eugene, Oregon 97408
www.harvesthousepublishers.com

ISBN 978-0-7369-7458-5 (pbk.)
ISBN 978-0-7369-7459-2 (eBook)

Library of Congress Cataloging-in-Publication Data

Names: Brodersen, Cheryl, 1960- author.
Title: A woman's battle for grace / Cheryl Brodersen.
Description: Eugene : Harvest House Publishers, 2018.
Identifiers: LCCN 2018011412 (print) | LCCN 2018015687 (ebook) | ISBN 9780736974592 (ebook) | ISBN 9780736974585 (pbk.)
Subjects: LCSH: Christian women--Religious life. | Grace (Theology)
Classification: LCC BV4527 (ebook) | LCC BV4527 .B746 2018 (print) | DDC 248.8/43--dc23
LC record available at https://lccn.loc.gov/2018011412

Printed in the United States of America

18 19 20 21 22 23 24 25 26 / VP-GL / 10 9 8 7 6 5 4 3 2 1

Contents

This book is dedicated to the author, source, and giver of grace, the Lord Jesus Christ, and to all those who find themselves in need of grace!

One

A Revelation of Grace

*By the grace of God I am what I am, and His grace toward
me was not in vain; but I labored more abundantly than they
all, yet not I, but the grace of God which was with me.*

1 CORINTHIANS 15:10

It started out as one of those perfect days. I walked around my perfectly ordered house, congratulating myself on a job well done.
I glanced at five neatly packed suitcases, ready for a lengthy missions trip to England with my husband and four children. My laundry was done, and dinner preparation was in full gear. On my bed
lay two masterful messages on grace I'd share the following day at
a women's conference at our home church. Though the pressure
to speak at a conference just two days before our scheduled departure would overwhelm others, it seemed to have no effect on me. I
remember my feelings of self-satisfied smugness as I contemplated
all my accomplishments.

If you hate me so far because of my perfect life, don't worry; it
was all about to change—drastically.

My husband, Brian, walked into the house with our teenage

daughter. They had left together that morning for Kristyn's visit to the hairdresser, and she'd been only mildly annoyed about her long, blond tresses. Now the same child was almost unrecognizable. Gone were the flowing locks, and in their place were inch-long spikes with concentric blond circles. I stared for a moment before my mind registered that I was looking at my daughter.

Then it happened. I let out a long and loud shriek! Unfortunately, that was only the beginning of my tirade. I can't remember how my daughter responded, but I know I let loose with a litany of comments a mother should never make to a daughter who is still in the throes of adolescence.

When my husband threw me the "Who are you and where did you come from?" look, I naturally turned my fury on him. How could he have allowed my daughter's hair to be plowed into these ghastly furrows?

That man then had the audacity to ask me if I was planning on speaking at the church the next day with "that attitude." Now the deepest reaches of my anger were loosed. I ran upstairs and grabbed my messages off the bed. Standing on the second floor overlooking the banister, I ripped them apart and poured their pieces down on astonished faces. Gone were the majestic messages extolling the glory of God's amazing grace.

Brian tried to calm me down, but his words only made me angrier. I ran back into my bedroom and loudly slammed the door behind me. Then it began to strike me that I, the woman who was supposed to share on amazing grace, was a monster. I desperately wanted the control I'd exhibited hours before my daughter's arrival home, but it wouldn't come. I threw myself on my knees and begged God to help me get control. I didn't want to be "that" woman I felt inside—the out-of-control woman who was scaring everyone around her.

Even as I prayed, I explained to the Lord that I was not "that" woman. I didn't even know her. She was nothing like the image I had of myself. Again, I repented. This time I asked the Lord to remove "that woman" from my home. I berated her. I hated her. Having sufficiently explained my case to the Lord and repented, I went out to apologize to the family. Five dismayed faces stared at me as I profusely apologized for my appalling behavior. I told them I'd been as shocked as they were by the irrational display of anger.

However, as I articulated my apology, the girl with the polka-dot-cropped hair said something sassy, and the beast came back to life! Back to my room I ran. I was as terrified of myself as my family was of me. I was out of control. I couldn't predict what I would do next. No one was safe, especially not me.

This time as I prayed I was crying and pleading with the Lord! I felt helpless against my own temper and irrationality. I told Him I wasn't getting off my knees or even leaving that room until He delivered me from myself. I was ready to feel the full condemnation of His disappointment with me; I had failed my family, my husband, the ministry, and the church. I had not only acted unbecomingly, but downright beastly. I fully deserved whatever sentence the Great Judge meted out. I was ready to step down from ministry as well as resign any position in the church He chose.

The message that came to me from the Lord was far different from the one I expected. First, it was kind. He reminded me of the story of Nebuchadnezzar found in Daniel 4, the humiliating experience of the prideful military conqueror and king of Babylon. Having had a troubling dream, he summoned the prophet Daniel to give him the interpretation. When Daniel heard the king's dream, he also became troubled and begrudgingly explained that the dream signified God was about to humble Nebuchadnezzar's pride in a drastic way. Daniel urged him to quickly humble himself before God so the episode could be avoided.

Nebuchadnezzar placed this saintly advice on the back burner. Perhaps he amended his way for a time, but he went right back to his prideful self. Then one day a year later, as he was perusing his kingdom and boasting to himself about his glorious accomplishments, the inevitable happened. Even as the prideful words spilled from Nebuchadnezzar's lips, a voice of judgment fell from heaven. At that very moment he lost all his senses and was driven to live among the beasts of the field until he acknowledged that the Most High ruled in the kingdom of men.

Like Nebuchadnezzar, I felt as though I had lost my sensibilities. I was totally out of control. Less than an hour before I had been walking in my own little kingdom of good works, congratulating myself on everything I'd done to merit God's grace. Now I felt the Lord speak to my heart, *Cheryl, this is you without My grace.* Immediately I began to cry out for God's grace to pour into, over, and on me. It did. This time, unlike the after of my other attempts, when I rose from my knees and left the room, the anger was gone. It hadn't simply subsided. It wasn't being suppressed. It wasn't even there. It was gone!

By the further grace of God, my family was able to not only forgive me, but to laugh with me as I retold the story of Nebuchadnezzar with me in the starring role. When I sat down with the Lord and my open Bible later that night, I received two entirely different messages on grace from the ones I had neatly typed and set on my bed. They contained no finger pointing and no example from my "perfect" life for how to display the quality of grace. No. This humbled pastor's wife shared the utter torment, beast-like qualities, and ugliness that happens when even for a moment God's grace is absent from our lives.

What a lesson I learned and shared that day! God wouldn't allow His amazing grace to be presented in a spirit of pride. Grace by its very nature is humble, offered to anyone who will receive it without regard to merit, accomplishments, or achievements. Grace is the great leveler for all mankind.

Growing Up Christian

Growing up in a Christian home, I thought I knew grace. I knew lots of Scriptures about grace. I loved the concept of grace—**G**od's **R**iches **A**t **C**hrist's **E**xpense. I loved to sing about grace, whether it was the rousing hymn "Wonderful Grace of Jesus" or the soul-filled words of John Newton's "Amazing Grace."

I grew up at a time when hippies were being saved and sharing startling and compelling testimonies of God's grace. However, until I felt the absence of God's grace on that day of insanity, I never truly realized how desperately dependent I was on this amazing and abundant gift from God. From that moment forward, I never wanted to experience a graceless moment again. In all honesty, however, I've had many more graceless experiences, but now I more quickly diagnose the problem and hurl myself on the ceaseless grace of Jesus. The other experiences haven't been as monumental, but they all taught me how slow I can be to realize my personal and constant need for God's grace and then to appropriate that grace for myself. Honestly, I've found it to be a constant battle to ascertain, accept, and then truly appropriate the grace of God.

It's funny how once you realize your need for something specific, it begins to stand out to you. It's like when you want a certain type of car, and suddenly you see that car every time you drive or park the jalopy you're presently driving. As I pored over the Scriptures in my personal devotions, or when I heard a Bible study, read a book, or sang a song with a reference to grace, it was as if lightning were striking. I began to see, as it were, a whole new battlefield in my life. At the center of the struggle was the great prize of a grace so much more abundant, precious, and powerful than I had ever imagined. If I were to truly receive and appropriate this great grace, I would need to enlist in the battle, learn the disciplines of grace, practice grace daily, and fight against my own personal enemies of grace.

I've heard when young men and women go to military boot camp, they're stripped of all their previous notions about war, pushed to extremes beyond themselves, and trained in new disciplines for battle. This is how the great soldiers who persevere in conflict and win the victory are forged. It's no different when you enlist in the battle for grace. You'll need to relinquish any preconceived concepts of grace that don't match the biblical definition. You'll be pushed beyond your natural capabilities into what can be accomplished only by grace. You'll need to be completely retrained and disciplined in the ways of God's amazing grace. You'll not only learn how desperately you need God's grace but how to lean into His grace in everything and for everything. Your identity will become synonymous with the army of grace, and by grace you will obtain the ultimate glory of grace.

Now, if after reading my experience your thoughts are, *Oh, Cheryl! Tsk! Tsk! Your behavior was abominable. I simply can't relate to you at all,* then perhaps this book is *not* for you. I'm not writing for the Mary Poppinses of this world—the women who can pull a measuring tape from their fully outfitted bags and announce, "Yes. That's me—practically perfect in every way." No!

This book is for those who

- struggle with condemnation.
- never seem to meet their own standards of perfection.
- feel overly burdened to meet the expectations of others.

- never feel as though they've done enough or done it well enough.
- constantly struggle with insecurities.
- are always trying to please others.
- feel substandard to other women.
- still deal with shame over the past.
- can't seem to conquer their temper.
- feel defeated.
- long to be a better person.
- want more spiritual power in their life.
- want to make a difference in their world.

If this is you, get ready for an induction into the battle for the marvelous grace of God.

The battle for grace is the good fight. It's the fight worth fighting. The prize is superior to and grander than anything you've ever fathomed. The victory has already been assured to you by the Champion of All Grace. Jesus trains our hands for war and leads the way in this conflict. He has supplied you, by grace, with everything you need to win the prize. Victory is near.

Are you ready to enlist? Do you desire to really understand and appropriate God's grace in your own life?

Before we enter the boot camp of grace, it's important to understand the prize we're fighting for. Without a cause, an army will lose a conflict. They need a purpose and a prize. To enlist in the battle for grace wholeheartedly, and therefore effectively, we need to define and elaborate on the stunningly lavish properties of grace. We'll do that in the next chapter. Once you begin to grasp an understanding of God's grace, I'm sure you'll be eager to enlist in the battle for grace.

Lord, please reveal Your amazing grace to me. Allow grace to be more than a far-off concept or lofty ideal. Grant me a fresh understanding of the exceeding grandeur and necessity of grace in my life. I ask this because of the exceeding riches of Your grace given to me through Your Son, Jesus Christ. In His name, amen.

For consideration:

1. Can you think of a time when you've felt the absence of God's grace?

2. What is your perception of grace?

3. Do you feel defeated, out of control, or helpless in any area of your life?

4. What draws you to know more about God's grace?

Two

What's So Great About Grace?

From his abundance we have all received one gracious blessing
after another. For the law was given through Moses, but God's
unfailing love and faithfulness came through Jesus Christ.

John 1:16-17 nlt

Would you like to know why grace is so amazing and the key to victory in your life? One of the most important facets to winning any battle is knowing the greatness of the objective you're fighting for. So to win the victory for grace, you must understand a bit about the glory of your objective.

During the Civil War in America, we're told, the Northern troops were losing when one day the emancipationist Julia Ward Howe overheard some of them going into battle singing "John Brown's Body." The tune was rousing, but the lyrics were depressing. She mentioned her dismay to the Reverend James Clarke, who suggested she write new lyrics to the familiar melody.

That night she went home and prayed, and in the middle of the night she was awakened with the lyrics of what has become known as the "The Battle Hymn of the Republic" coursing through her mind. In Julia's own recollection of the experience, the words simply and divinely flowed from her pen onto the paper.[1]

> Mine eyes have seen the glory of the coming of the
>   Lord:
> He is trampling out the vintage where the grapes of
>   wrath are stored;
> He hath loosed the fateful lightning of His terrible
>   swift sword:
> His truth is marching on.
>
> I have seen Him in the watch-fires of a hundred cir-
>   cling camps,
> They have builded Him an altar in the evening dews
>   and damps;
> I can read His righteous sentence by the dim and flar-
>   ing lamps:
> His day is marching on.
>
> He has sounded forth the trumpet that shall never
>   call retreat;
> He is sifting out the hearts of men before His
>   judgment-seat;
> O, be swift, my soul, to answer Him! Be jubilant, my
>   feet!
> Our God is marching on.
>
> In the beauty of the lilies Christ was born across the
>   sea,
> With a glory in His bosom that transfigures you and
>   me:
> As He died to make men holy, let us die to make men
>   free,
> While God is marching on.

Chorus: Glory! Glory! Hallelujah! His truth is
    marching on.

It's been said this song changed the course of the war because it
inspired the Northern troops to victory by reminding them of the
glory of their cause.

Grace is as great a cause as emancipation, because grace is divine
emancipation and blessing. But how can such a glorious objective
be described? Grace is so glorious and so divine that it takes a myriad of definitions just to attempt to understand it.

Grace for Grace

A group of us was ready to have a delicious Mexican meal after
Sunday morning services. The only table available for a party of
eight in the restaurant was in a corner by a large-screen television.
I was able to ignore most of the scenes that flashed on the screen—
until a certain hair straightener was demonstrated. I lost all awareness of the conversations around me and became mesmerized. The
transformation of all the different hair types was amazing. With one
lingering stroke of the gizmo, a woman's curly hair turned into spun
silk. Then another model's unruly hair became perfectly coiffured.
Moving on, a woman with stick-straight hair suddenly sported lux-
uriant curls.

I realized I needed this gizmo in my life. My *hair* needed this
gizmo! Before I'd walked into that restaurant, before I'd taken a bite
of my cheese enchilada, I hadn't known I had such a need in my life.
I hadn't even known it was possible to so easily change the disposition of my hair. But now that I knew, I wanted that gizmo. I pulled
a pen out of my purse and grabbed the nearest napkin. Turning to
my friends, who were staring at me in perplexity, I explained that
the item advertised on the TV intrigued me. They watched with me

as I waited to copy the phone number and website so I could purchase this amazing tool.

Just then they announced it—the deal got better! No longer would only the gizmo come into my possession if I called the number; there would be more. Along with the straightener I would get the world's best hairbrush. Oh, but that wasn't all. They would also throw in some beautiful hair clips. And if I called within the next 15 minutes, they would slash the price to a mere half of what other retailers were charging for a similar item. I was hooked!

Most of us have seen the same type of offer again and again, but because they're rarely the great deal they're advertised to be, we've grown leery of anything that seems too good to be true.

So it is with many Christians. They live outside the realm of grace because it simply seems too good to be true. They constantly live under the tyranny of trying to be good enough to merit God's favor. The abundant life Jesus promised is reduced to the drudgery of trying to follow rules, regulations, and rituals, which is no abundant life at all.

Yet grace offers us an even better deal. Yes, I've enjoyed my gizmo and the brush and the hairclips that came with it, but that pales in comparison to the presence of the great and amazing grace I've received through Christ Jesus. As with the gizmo advertised on television, I hadn't realized how desperately I needed this grace until I began to see it applied to the life of people I knew. When I saw its transforming effect on others, I knew I had to have it!

Grace is so enormously wonderful that those who have experienced it struggle to define it. What can we say about grace?

- Grace is much more than an attitude or a disposition,
  yet it's an attitude of kindness and generosity.

- Grace is even more than simply God's favor, yet it's God's active goodness and attention riveted on us.

- Grace is more than merely a power, yet grace contains substantial power.

- Grace is more than God's forgiveness, yet through it we are freely forgiven.

- Grace is more than God's riches through Christ, yet it contains God's richest blessings through Christ.

- Grace is more than salvation, yet it's through God's grace that we are saved.

- Grace is more than God canceling our past sin and remembering it no more, yet it's by grace that God cancels our sins and buries them in the deepest sea.

- Grace is more than God's willingness to overlook our faults and deficiencies, yet it's because of God's grace that He overlooks our faults and deficiencies.

What is grace? It's all the above and more!

The Attitude of Grace

I remember my daughter Kristyn's frustration when she was five years old and learning to ride a bike. We took her out to the cul-de-sac in front of our house and ceremoniously removed her training wheels. Kristyn felt ready to ride like a big girl, and she smiled as she climbed onto the seat. Her father held the bike steady and ran with her as she pedaled in big circles. But her confidence waned the moment her daddy let go, and she took one tumble after another.

Her three-year-old brother watched from the sidelines. After helping her up after a fall, he commandeered her bike. "Watch me!"

he coached as he climbed on and began to perfectly maneuver the small pink bike. Kristyn was not amused! She'd tried so hard to follow all the biking rules she'd learned, but that made her overly self-aware and cautious. This also prohibited her from simply enjoying the freedom of riding her bike. Her little brother, on the other hand, had never had training wheels, never learned the bike rules, and never had the awareness that he could fall. He simply grabbed the bike and rode.

Did we scold Kristyn after she fell? No way! We congratulated her and praised her for trying. Did we give up on teaching her to ride a bike? No! We kept working with her until she gained the confidence and skill to ride the bike all by herself. When the day came that she could independently climb on that bike and ride like a pro, her father and I shouted and cheered!

I would describe our attitude toward Kristyn as gracious. It was one of patience, love, kindness, and perseverance. At the forefront of our hearts were Kristyn's welfare and joy.

God's attitude toward us is even more gracious! He's dedicated to giving us the abundant life He promised. Jesus said, "'I have come that they may have life, and that they may have it more abundantly'" (John 10:10). When Jesus spoke these words, He wasn't just talking about a quantity of life but a quality of life. Again, the Gospel of John records Jesus saying, "'These things I have spoken to you, that My joy may remain in you, and that your joy may be full'" (John 15:11).

God is the ultimate Father, a good Father who's interested in the welfare and joy of His children. He looks on us with absolute kindness. The psalmist made note of this in Psalm 103:13-14: "As a father pities his children, so the LORD pities those who fear Him. For He knows our frame; He remembers that we are dust."

So many have the mistaken and unbiblical notion that God is

waiting—and wanting—for us to mess up. They picture Him eager to have some excuse to disqualify us from His grace. However, grace by its very essence means beneficence, or goodness. It's the attitude God constantly displays toward us. He's deeply interested in our welfare. He's for our ultimate best. To give us His best, God sent Jesus to pay the penalty our sin deserved so we could receive the lavish blessings He desires to pour out on His children. That's one reason grace is worth fighting for!

God's Grace Is Favor

In the Bible, the word *grace* is often translated "favor." In Luke 1:28 the angel Gabriel greeted Mary by saying, "'Rejoice, highly favored one, the Lord is with you.'" He was also saying, "Rejoice, highly *graced* one, the Lord is with you." Mary's favor came because God was aware of her and had chosen to bring through her life His greatest treasure—Jesus.

Mary probably felt ordinary or maybe even oppressed. She lived in an obscure village the notables of Jewish society looked down on. She was engaged to what today we'd call a blue-collar worker— a carpenter. Though she was of the lineage of David, as was her fiancé, Joseph, such a heritage was a liability. The Roman government, King Herod, and the family of the high priest were threatened by the prophecies of the eternal monarch who would arise from the dynasty of David. Mary's country was under the oppressive rule of Rome. She was, in her self-description, of "lowly state" (Luke 1:48).

Until the moment of Gabriel's visitation, Mary may not have realized the favor she held with God. God had been watching, observing, and making plans to bless and exalt Mary's life. Mary described this grace in her song of praise when she said, "'Behold, henceforth all generations will call me blessed. For He who is mighty has done great things for me'" (verses 48-49). Then she prophetically offered this same grace to any who would fear the Lord: "'And His mercy is on those who fear Him from generation to generation'" (verse 50).

Do you desire to know the favor of God on your life? Mary came to know it through the angelic announcement. However, through the Word of God, we, too, can be assured that God's grace is on our lives. This is why the apostle Paul began every one of his letters with a greeting almost identical to "Grace and peace from God our Father and the Lord Jesus Christ." Grace and peace is our heavenly greeting and our constant assurance! The grace on Mary's life allowed her to conceive in her and bring forth Jesus into the world. This miraculous process took place when the Holy Spirit came "upon" her and "the power of the Highest" overshadowed her (Luke 1:35). In the same way, God favors us so we can have Jesus living in us, and then we, too, can present the life of Jesus to the world.

The knowledge that she was favored sustained Mary through many hardships, threats, and perplexities. We're told she "pondered" and "treasured" these things in her heart (Luke 2:19 KJV; Luke 2:51 NLT). Her life wasn't easy or exalted. Her morality and godliness were doubted. Rome imposed taxes upon her fiancé. In her ninth month of pregnancy, she had to travel over 90 difficult miles to the overcrowded village of Bethlehem. There she gave birth to her firstborn, the Messiah, in a stable surrounded by animals because there was no room for them in the inn (Luke 2:1-7). When the child Jesus was still young, she had to flee with her family to Egypt to escape the threat of the murderous King Herod. After the death of Herod, she and her family settled in Nazareth because of a new threat from Herod's son (Matthew 2:13-15). Mary endured all these circumstances with the knowledge that God's favor was upon her.

We all desire the assurance of God's favor. However, our circumstances might tempt us to deny this radical truth. Yes, we must battle to recognize God's favor on our lives when circumstances threaten to tell us otherwise. If we don't realize God's favor, we'll walk in defeat rather than in purpose, wisdom, and victory!

God's Grace Is Power

Grace is God's power working in us. This is a concept we will explore in greater detail in another chapter. However, I want to whet your appetite just a bit. In Ephesians 3:7, Paul described grace as the "effective working" of God's power given to him. Grace is God's infusion of spiritual power to do what we can't do naturally. God never intended for us to try to live the Christian life in our own strength. If the abundant life were doable in our own strength, we would have little or no need for God. The fact is He calls us to a life that is spiritually, physically, mentally, and emotionally impossible without the power of His grace working in and through us. This spiritual power is so great, so perfectly sufficient for every need, that it's worth the battle to experience it!

God's Grace Is Forgiveness

Grace is the means by which God has forgiven our sins. The basis of our forgiveness now rests in our faith in Jesus Christ, not in the sacrifices we offer, the rituals we observe, or the methodologies we practice. Paul stated in Ephesians 1:7, "In Him we have redemption through His blood, the forgiveness of sins, according to the riches of His grace." Did you see that? Our forgiveness is because of what Jesus has done for us, not what we have done for Jesus. That's grace!

The word *forgiveness* means to cancel a debt. Nothing is more emancipating than when a debt against us is canceled! This is exactly what God, in His grace through Christ Jesus, has done for us. We didn't deserve to be forgiven. We didn't earn forgiveness. It was given to us. Jesus Christ lived the perfect and sinless life we should have lived. Then Jesus suffered the death our sins deserved. The wages of our sin, the just penalty for the sins we commit, is death. Jesus canceled that debt by dying in our place. That's grace!

Have you ever owed a great debt? Perhaps you broke the law? When I was 19, I received a traffic ticket I justly deserved. I waited anxiously for the letter that would tell me the cost and requirement to deal with my infraction. When it arrived, I learned the cost would be determined at a court hearing.

My father agreed to appear before the judge with me. I felt so much guilt. I'd been on a road trip and was giddy in the company of friends. I'd been speeding, unaware of how fast I was driving. The police officer who pulled me over was truly gracious. According to California's laws he could have taken me to jail, but he let me go with a ticket.

The court appointment came, and my father drove with me to the Ventura courthouse, about 70 miles from where we lived. He even took a day off from work. We had to go to a certain counter and register. We waited in line, hoping to just pay the debt and leave, while the woman looked for the right document. Dad pulled out his checkbook. I'd had no idea he planned to pay my debt for me. The lady returned and said I would have to appear before the judge.

We entered the designated courtroom. My only solace was my father's presence next to me. I was shaking. He reached over, took my hand, and held it tightly until my name was called. As I moved forward to stand before the judge, Dad took a seat closer to the front of the courtroom so he could be near me.

As the judge looked down at the charges, he began to justly scold me. Had I been going even five miles faster he would have thrown me in jail for three nights. He said, "Even right now, as I look at you, I am tempted to throw you in jail as a good lesson." Tears poured down my face. My whole frame was wrecked. Then the judge pronounced a monetary price for the penalty of my crime and dismissed me.

While I was being chastised, my father had already been filling out the check, and then he wrote in the amount required to pay for my violation. He stood up immediately to escort me out of court. As he did so he whispered, "It's over, baby! You're free now!"

Although Dad had been kind throughout the whole experience, I still expected a strong lecture or even a good berating over the stupidity, expense, and dangers of speeding. That's not what happened. Instead he talked about the vacation we would soon be taking and all the great things we'd do.

My dad was a man who knew the grace of God, and he showed me grace that day. It's a grace worth fighting for!

God's Grace Is Blessing

We've already talked about how grace is God's riches at Christ's expense. If this were the only definition of grace, it would be glorious. Grace is the free flow of God's blessings to us because Jesus dealt with the obstacles to those blessings.

Our God is a God of blessings. When He established the nation of Israel, He commanded the priests to put His blessing on the people. Do you know what that blessing included? You guessed it! His grace.

> The LORD bless you and keep you;
> The LORD make His face shine upon you,
> And be gracious to you;
> The LORD lift up His countenance upon you,
> And give you peace (Numbers 6:24-26).

God desires to bless us. It's in His very nature to bless. Ephesians

1:3 informs us He "has blessed us with every spiritual blessing in the heavenly places in Christ." God desires to bless our lives by reason of His grace. He wants to lavish on us all the blessings Jesus deserves. Psalm 84:11 states, "The Lord God is a sun and shield; the Lord will give grace and glory; no good thing will He withhold from those who walk uprightly."

Take a moment to think through this reality with me. God is all-powerful. He has no impossibilities. He is Creator God. The evidence of His workmanship is visible all around us in the beauty of the sky, trees, plants, fruit, flowers, mountains, hills, birds, animals, oceans, lakes, rivers, and streams. As His creation, we're naturally drawn to beauty, whether the beauty of a landscape or a human being. We love to observe it.

Recently Brian and I stayed in a room with a view of the Mediterranean Sea. Every night we sat on our balcony and watched the spectacle of God's artwork as the sun dipped into the water. Oh, it was glorious! We were transfixed by its beauty. This God of creation and beauty is determined to bless our lives. He desires to infuse us with the manifestation of His grace. Now, isn't it worth fighting to have the blessing of God on our lives?

God's Grace Is Salvation

Safe to say, we, as fallen humanity, did not deserve the grace of God that saved us. Read Paul's description of our fallen condition from Ephesians 2:1-3:

> You He made alive, who were dead in trespasses and
> sins, in which you once walked according to the
> course of this world, according to the prince of the
> power of the air, the spirit who now works in the
> sons of disobedience, among whom also we all once

conducted ourselves in the lusts of our flesh, fulfilling
the desires of the flesh and of the mind, and were by
nature children of wrath, just as the others.

God desired to extend the grace of salvation to this lost humanity. This salvation didn't come by the result of men recognizing their lost condition, crying out for help, or even wanting to be saved. It was "God, who is rich in mercy, because of His great love with which He loved us, even when we were dead in trespasses, made us alive together with Christ (by grace you have been saved)" (Ephesians 2:4-5).

God was the initiator. God was moved by His grace to save man. His plan of salvation had to appease His righteousness and His love. His righteousness demanded a penalty against rebellion and sin. His love compelled Him to rescue rebels and sinners. God appeased both demands through the sacrifice of His righteous Son, Jesus. Jesus, as the Son of God, volunteered to wage war against sin and gave His righteous life to pay the penalty mankind's sins incurred. This was the ultimate act of grace, but not the last. Through this act of saving grace, all the great grace of God can be realized, known, and experienced. Isn't that a grace worth fighting for?

God's Grace Cancels Our Sin

How often have you heard someone say, "I might forgive you, but I will never forget what you've done"? What does that mean? It means the person who committed the wrong will forever be identified by the wrong he did. He might not have to pay the penalty, but the stain will always be visible. Not so with God! God promises to forgive our sins and remember them no more. In prophesying the New Covenant God would make through the Messiah, the prophet Jeremiah mentions this amazing provision: "'I will forgive their iniquity, and their sin I will remember no more'" (Jeremiah 31:34). It's wonderful to have the debt of sin canceled and paid in full. It's even more glorious to never be associated with that sin again.

As a young girl, I had the privilege of hearing Corrie ten Boom speak from the podium in the main sanctuary at my father's church. She was the Dutch Christian who helped many Jews escape the Nazi Holocaust during World War II by hiding them in her closet, and then was imprisoned. It was not uncommon for her to come to church and take a seat in the front row. Whenever my father saw her, he was sure she had a word to share with the congregation, and he inevitably invited her to take the pulpit and speak.

On more than one occasion Corrie reminded us of this divine faculty of God to "remember our sins no more," quoting Micah 7:18-19: "Who is a God like You, pardoning iniquity and passing over the transgression of the remnant of His heritage? He does not retain His anger forever, because He delights in mercy. He will again have compassion on us, and will subdue our iniquities. You will cast all our sins into the depths of the sea." After reading this Scripture she would look at all the people gathered and announce, "God throws our sin into the deepest sea and then places a sign over it saying, 'No fishing!'"

God refuses to identify us by our past. He makes all things new. He gives us fresh and bright beginnings. Second Corinthians 5:17 is a familiar but powerful text that reminds us of this truth. "If anyone is in Christ, he is a new creation; old things have passed away; behold, all things have become new." So not only is the debt of sin canceled, but our evil doings are forgotten. That's amazing grace, don't you think?

A friend of mine was constantly troubled until she had a divine revelation. Before she was saved, she lived a turbulent life, which included nine abortions. She struggled to forgive and forget her own past. Then one day. as she was reading about God's forgiveness, she paused on the passage in Micah 7:18-19 and prayed, *God, if You forget, why do I remember?*

The Spirit of the Lord spoke to her and said, *I allow you to remember so you don't forget the damage caused by your old lifestyle and return to it. However, I have chosen never to remember it or call it to mind!* What a comfort that became to her. Whenever she was reminded of her past, she used it as a catalyst to thank God for all He delivered her from and to keep her from ever returning to those old ways.

Isn't this new identity a grace worth fighting for?

God's Grace Overlooks Our Failures

Grace puts the expectation on God, not on us. The psalmist realized this when he said, "O my soul, you have said to the LORD, 'You are my Lord, my goodness is nothing apart from You'" (Psalm 16:2). Paul realized this when he wrote, "I know that in me (that is, in my flesh), nothing good dwells; for to will is present with me, but how to perform what is good I do not find" (Romans 7:18). Most importantly, Jesus said, "'I am the vine, you are the branches. He who abides in Me, and I in him, bears much fruit; for without Me you can do nothing'" (John 15:5).

So much more can be said on this subject, so we'll explore it in another chapter. However, I mention it now to tantalize your appetite with the graciousness of grace. God knows our frame. He knows our weaknesses. He knows our great intentions and our inability to carry them through to the end. Part of God's grace is His divine patience with us. He is like a Father who doesn't put unreal expectations on His children.

When I was training to be a teacher years ago, I read a book on age-appropriate expectations. It highlighted what children, based on their age, were capable of learning and absorbing. Certain concepts are more readily grasped at certain ages than others. For example, at five, children can learn to recognize letters and their sounds and read. Because of the underdevelopment of their hand muscles, however, they aren't ready to learn cursive writing. It was important, as a teacher, not to put unreal expectations on my students.

At one point Jesus said to His disciples, "'I still have many things to say to you, but you cannot bear them now'" (John 16:12). Jesus knew what the disciples were ready for and what they were not ready for. He didn't berate them for their inability to grasp the "many things" He wanted to say to them. He would wait until they were mature and experienced enough to receive them.

Mercy is a way of defining this characteristic of covering our faults and failures. God doesn't disqualify us when we fail. He knows our weaknesses and compensates for them with His grace. Psalm 103:11-14 speaks about this very issue: "As the heavens are high above the earth, so great is His mercy toward those who fear Him; as far as the east is from the west, so far has He removed our transgressions from us. As a father pities his children, so the LORD pities those who fear Him. For He knows our frame; He remembers that we are dust."

Isn't God's mercy something to fight for?

When I talk about fighting, I'm echoing Paul's commission to Timothy: "Fight the good fight of faith" (1 Timothy 6:12). There is such a thing as a good fight. A good fight is a cause worthy of all our efforts and discipline. It's worth all the opposition and animosity. It's worth the exertion. It's worth the time. It's worth the dedication. It's worth the fight, because grace is the riches of God lavished on us through Christ Jesus.

Did you notice that all these attributes of grace belong to God?

That's because grace is exclusive to God. We put too many expectations on ourselves. Grace is not natural to our nature. We might have bits of grace, acknowledge our need for grace, or even admire the beauty of grace, but that's because even in our fallen images we still bear residual characteristics of the image of God. The actual source of all grace is God.

The apostle Peter makes this clear when he states God is the God of all grace. First Peter 5:10 (NIV) says, "The God of all grace, who called you to his eternal glory in Christ, after you have suffered a little while, will himself restore you and make you strong, firm and steadfast." We can find and receive this marvelous grace in only one place—in the throne room of grace. Our heavenly Father longs to infuse our lives with this grace so others will see the magnificent grace of Jesus through us. Don't you long to be more than you are? Don't you want this divine grace operating in your life?

....

Dear Lord, open my eyes to behold the wonders of Your grace. Show me the riches of what You desire me to have and hold through Christ Jesus. Remove all my misconceptions about grace and replace them with truths found in Your Word. Give me eyes to see, ears to hear, meekness to receive, and an understanding heart to believe. Thank You for the amazing grace You have richly bestowed on me through Christ Jesus. In Jesus's name, amen!

For consideration:

1. What misconceptions have you held about grace?
2. How is grace even more than you thought?

3. Which aspect of grace do you need to appropriate the most?

4. Read Psalm 103 and write down all the gifts of God's grace you discover.

5. List three reasons God's grace is worth fighting for.

Three

The Battle

Let us therefore come boldly to the throne of grace, that we may obtain mercy and find grace to help in time of need.

HEBREWS 4:16

I was born in 1960, a time when television was becoming part of every American household. I still remember the day I went with my dad to buy a color television set to replace our black and white one. He bought it used from a man who refurbished broken TVs and resold them from his garage. Mom set it up downstairs in our family room, and it immediately became an important family fixture.

What I remember most about watching television in my youth are the commercials and their jingles. "Curlers in your hair—shame on you" or "Ring around the collar!" It seemed that most of the advertisers sought to embarrass or shame the audience into buying their product.

One coffee commercial depicted a couple visiting their neighbor. The wife was astounded when her husband asked the neighbor for a second cup of coffee. She followed the hostess into the kitchen, dismayed. Her spouse had never wanted a second cup of her own coffee. There in the kitchen, her hostess showed her why. She'd been using the wrong coffee! The next scene showed the wife, having changed her brand of coffee, pouring a second cup of coffee for her husband and smiling at the camera, content.

Other commercials made us self-conscious about the toothpaste, shaving cream, shampoo, soap, dishwashing liquid, and even the laundry detergent we were using.

Those of you close to my age might remember the 1978 perfume commercial with a gorgeous woman, perfectly coiffured and dressed to the nines, proudly singing, "I can bring home the bacon, fry it up in a pan, and never let you forget you're a man!"[1] This "24-hour woman" was who every American woman was supposed to aspire to be. She could do and be everything! She could be successful at work, cook a great meal, and be alluring to her husband, all the time looking perfectly put together!

These types of commercials misshaped the self-image of many children growing up. The pressure was on to buy the right product, use the right product, and live up to the claims of that product. Whew! Such demands left consumers disillusioned, dissatisfied, and demoralized. No product could fill the void that everyone had and has for acceptance, contentment, and fulfillment.

During this era the professionals began to weigh in on how to conduct every area of life. Dr. Spock told parents the right way and the wrong way to raise their children. Adelle Davis instructed people on the healthy way to eat. Jack LaLanne daily led audiences through a series of calisthenics to strengthen their muscles. Graham Kerr and Julia Child took over our kitchens with their creative recipes and expertise. As this new era began, women started questioning everything they'd been doing in the home.

Every day we hear stories that tell us we don't measure up. Life has always been a battle, but even more so in the culture where we find ourselves. A myriad of self-help books instruct us on the correct way to order every area of our lives, drawing heavily on the need to retrain ourselves, discipline ourselves, and put extra effort into doing what we do. The truth is we're already pressed for time, we know we could do better, and we're shamed into feeling guilty over our failed attempts at perfection. The intimidation we feel makes us try harder, yet leaves us with even more insecurities.

One of the greatest battles the world has ever witnessed took place in Kinshasa, Zaire, in October 1974. There in a stadium with 60,000 people, Mohammed Ali fought challenger George Foreman for the title of World Heavy Weight Champion. Both men were in peak condition, and George Foreman, as the younger fighter, was predicted to win. While both men were training in Zaire weeks before the bout, however, Ali began a campaign of intimidation. Every day he walked two tigers down the street in front of Foreman's hotel. Ali used this ploy to show off his incredible strength, control, and fearlessness. Mohammed was already throwing psychological punches at Foreman before the two men even entered the ring.

Whether or not this mental maneuver contributed to George Foreman's knockout in the eighth round and Mohammed Ali's subsequent victory, no one can say for certain. However, it lends proof to the claim that a large part of every battle is intimidation. The final outcome might be determined in the boxing ring, but the fight begins long before the boxing gloves are put on.

So what is the battle we're facing? It's the battle for grace. The resources of grace are already there. Our battle is in getting to the grace place and appropriating the grace God has for us. Whether or not you realize it, the battle is raging around you and within you. The Enemy is employing all sorts of tactics to cut off your ammunition supplies. The battle is waged on all sorts of fronts. It's psychological. The Enemy wants you to think there's no throne room of grace, or that you don't have the right credentials to gain access to it. At other times he wants to scare you away from the throne room of grace. He presents it as something other than what it is or tells you better ammunition supplies are elsewhere.

At other times the battle takes on physical proportions. You get distracted. You get busy. Although you're running low on motivation, love, kindness, energy, and strength, you're so focused on all the work you need to do that you neglect the throne room of grace. Distraction is one of the Enemy's greatest weapons to keep us from the throne room of grace. You must keep the objective of grace always in sight. An army needs weapons and supplies if they're going to win the war. You need to get to the storehouse of grace if you're going to win the battle for grace. If you're going to see, feel, and experience the power of grace operating in your life, you must keep the roads to grace clear.

Don't Let Intimidation Stop You

As recipients of grace, we face many battles to getting grace, keeping grace, and maintaining grace. We run out of grace and constantly need to refortify our supply. Again, the Enemy wants to keep us from that powerhouse.

One of the tactics he uses to keep us from the grace place is intimidation. We, in our natural state, are not strong enough to ignore the taunts and insults of the Enemy. We succumb to insecurity and intimidation. We draw back. We insulate. We're afraid, because deep in our hearts we know we're not strong enough, wise enough, courageous enough, good enough, or tough enough to win the battles of life. Ah, but this is where grace becomes our greatest ally. Grace is the ample supply of a divine sufficiency to persevere against every tactic of the Enemy and valiantly triumph over these same tactics.

The objective of the Enemy is to take our eyes from God's grace and rivet them to our own meager supplies and fractured humanity. Why? Because grace is the divine arsenal from which we gather all our ammunition for every conflict. Grace brings the sufficiency of God's power to every conflict. The Enemy wants to cut you off from this powerful supply line.

What would have happened if David had listened to and believed the taunts of Goliath? No doubt he would have focused on the giant's threats, intimidating size, military successes, and seemingly impenetrable armament. Had David allowed these things to distract him, he never would have volunteered to face Goliath. Obviously, these distractions kept the other soldiers and the king himself from battling the giant, but David's attention was riveted to the God of Israel. Because of this, Goliath's taunts fell on deaf ears.

No favorable comparison can be made between the shepherd boy and the hero of the Philistines. David didn't measure his strength against Goliath's strength. He didn't measure his military experience against Goliath's military background. He didn't measure his weapons against Goliath's. He didn't measure Goliath's size (a giant's) against his own (a mere lad's). No. David measured Goliath next to God, and Goliath fell short.

David said to the giant,

> "You come to me with a sword, with a spear, and with a javelin. But I come to you in the name of the LORD of hosts, the God of the armies of Israel, whom you have defied. This day the LORD will deliver you into my hand, and I will strike you and take your head from you... that all the earth may know that there is

a God in Israel. Then all the assembly shall know that
the LORD does not save with sword and spear; for the
battle is the LORD's, and He will give you into our
hands" (1 Samuel 17:45-47).

David was able to push through all the intimidation of the
enemy and tap into the powerful grace of God because he gave the
battle to God! He realized the victory was not determined by size,
experience, weapons, or words, but by the power of God.

The only way to push past intimidation and into the throne
room of grace is to recognize the power, compassion, and majesty of
the One who sits on the throne. Remember, this powerful giant was
felled by one stone from a shepherd's bag. Grace is like that one little stone. It hits the giants of intimidation in our lives right between
the eyes and renders them helpless. No wonder the Enemy wants
to keep you from grace!

Don't Let Deficits Keep You Out

I hate deficits. As I age, I'm feeling more and more the deficit of strength and energy. I have often been dismayed at the deficit of money in our bank account to meet mounting bills. Almost
daily I experience the deficit of time. We all have felt the deficits of
skill, experience, and strength. Too often, rather than recognizing
and admitting these deficits and making our way to the throne of
grace, we try to compensate for them, ignore them, or find another
source to fill them.

I remember an event in my life for which I felt totally unpre-
pared. I was undone. The circumstances seemed unmanageable and
way beyond my skill set. I presented the situation in prayer with the
women I regularly pray with on Tuesday mornings. Suddenly this
Scripture from John 6:6 came to mind: "[Jesus] Himself knew what

He would do." I was overwhelmed with the realization that Jesus had allowed these circumstances in my life. In fact, it was Jesus who drew my attention to the deficit and my inability to fix it. Why had He done this? Because He had a plan! He already knew what He was going to do. He was driving me into the throne room of grace so I could have a front-row seat to behold His grace at work. After prayer I went back to the story in John 6.

As Philip sat near Jesus on the hillside overlooking the Sea of Galilee, the day began to wane. A multitude of 5000 men, along with their spouses and children, continued to mill around the presence of Jesus. Suddenly Jesus turned to Philip and asked, "'Where shall we buy bread, that these may eat?'" (John 6:5). In that instant Philip became aware of all the deficits around him. The hour was late, so there was a deficit of time. The only food available was a lad's lunch of two fish and five small barley loaves. This meant a deficit of food. Philip commented to Jesus that even a year's wages would not be enough to purchase bread for the entire crowd to eat. That meant a deficit of money, and besides, the stores were quite a distance away. Then there was the great deficit of the appetite of the multitude.

I have often wondered if Philip was aware of this deficit before Jesus drew his attention to it. This is not the end of the story, though. The cause for hope is found in John 6:6: "But this He said to test him, for He Himself knew what He would do." Jesus was measuring Philip's grace supply. It was low!

Jesus knew what He was about to do. He was about to fill the deficit to overflowing. He received the lad's lunch, directed the disciples to organize the crowd into groups of 50, and blessed the meager meal. Then Jesus broke the bread into pieces and filled basket after basket. He did the same with the fish. The baskets were given to the disciples to distribute to the crowd. John records that everyone ate as much as they wanted, and they still had 12 baskets of leftovers!

The throne room of grace never has deficits, although God will often use deficits to move you into His presence. Intimidation doesn't have to keep you outside the throne room of grace. You can use intimidation as a catalyst to drive you there!

To have a constant supply of grace, we must constantly keep the access open to the divine supply. This means we must ignore, shut out, refuse to pay attention to, and resist being distracted by the taunts of the Enemy. We then use those very same intimidators to drive us into the throne room. How is that possible? By a daily trek to the throne of grace so we can receive grace to help in the time of need! By habitually making our way to this divine haven, we keep the path clear. Hebrews 4:16 says, "Let us therefore come boldly to the throne of grace, that we may obtain mercy and find grace to help in the time of need." This is the very supply the Enemy would like to cut you off from.

Enter Boldly

Note that Hebrews 4:16 implores us to come "boldly" to the throne of grace. Intimidation wants to rob you of that boldness. It stands outside the door and tries to disqualify you from entering. Intimidation tells you all the reasons you don't deserve entrance into the throne room of grace. One of the strengths of this intimidation is the fact that we know we're not worthy of an appointment before the High King of heaven. We're well aware of our own shortcomings and failures. Grace by its very nature, however, welcomes the disqualified. That's right. Grace qualifies the disqualified by the qualifications of Jesus. We enter not on our own merit, but on and by the merits of Jesus's perfection, accomplishments, and command! The name of Jesus is what gives us bold entrance. He is the password to the throne room of grace.

I boldly enter this divine room because of my relationship with the Son of God. Because of Jesus I'm gladly welcomed into this Holy of Holies of God's presence. I am thoroughly qualified by Christ. He has removed all the disqualifiers my sin marred me with. He then qualified me by His righteousness. The New Living Translation states 2 Corinthians 5:21 like this: "God made Christ, who never sinned, to be the offering for our sin, so that we could be made right with God through Christ."

Nothing is quite like a bold entrance, but a bold entrance is only possible when you know all the requirements have been met, that you're wanted, that you're loved, and that you're expected. It's like going home for Christmas. I never hesitated to enter my parents' house on Christmas morning. I had the key my father gave me, and I knew I was wanted and loved by those who lived in the house. Add to that the fact that my arrival was expected. The thought of being excluded from my father's house never even crossed my mind.

So, too, you're welcomed in the throne room of grace. Your name is known there. You're wanted there. You're loved there. Your presence is expected. God is waiting there to meet with you and supply you with all the grace you need. The Christian life was never meant to be lived with only our meager human reserves. Isaiah 30:18 states that God waits for us so He can be gracious to us.

> Therefore the LORD will wait, that He may be gracious to you; and therefore He will be exalted, that He may have mercy on you. For the LORD is a God of justice; blessed are all those who wait for Him.

God is waiting for us to enter His throne room of grace so He might give to us all the grace we need from the great storehouses of His grace.

Approach the Throne of Grace

With this bold confidence we enter the throne room of grace and approach a throne of grace. That's right. Our divine supply is issued from the throne of grace. It's not a throne of demands or intimidation, but one of welcome, accessibility, and gentleness. From the throne of grace God dispenses grace.

From Exodus 13:21-22, we know when the children of Israel were delivered from Egypt, God gave them a pillar of cloud to cover them by day, and this same cloud became a pillar of fire at night. During the day the cloud insulated them from the scorching heat of the sun. It gave them shade and moisture in the arid wilderness. At night the pillar of fire provided warmth in the frigid desert and light to see by.

We read in Exodus 14:19-20, however, that this same cloud that provided divine grace to Israel enshrouded the enemy camp in darkness "so that the one did not come near the other all that night." God gave Israel exactly what they needed for their pilgrimage through the wilderness. He filled every deficit Israel had with His divine supply of grace. God also allowed Israel to know deficit so they might realize His divine supply of grace. Deuteronomy 8:3 says,

> So He humbled you, allowed you to hunger, and fed
> you with manna which you did not know nor did
> your fathers know, that He might make you know
> that man shall not live by bread alone; but man lives
> by every word that proceeds from the mouth of the
> Lord.

Through their wilderness experience Israel learned that God would meet every deficit with His divine supply. Philip learned that Jesus could amply overcome any and every deficit of the multitude with His majestic grace. So as you enter the throne room of God's grace, you will be met with the supply of sufficiency for whatever deficit you have.

To those who have a relationship with Jesus Christ, the throne room of God is always open. It accepts everyone who comes through the beloved Son of God, who lived a righteous life and died an atoning death for all mankind. For those who know Jesus, the throne room is an insulation, a protection, a refuge, and a storehouse for a myriad of graces.

Find Grace

Here in this room we find the divine supply to valiantly fight the battle for grace. We fight for grace by grace. We receive and employ God's grace to overcome every need, difficulty, and deficiency. This is our divine supply for everything life throws at us. Here is all the wisdom, all the motivation, all the strength, and all the power we need to be victorious.

This is the only source of grace, with no other supply and no other location. God is the source of grace, and His throne room is the supply room. He is the God of All Grace (1 Peter 5:10). He is the creator of grace, and He alone holds the abundant supply we need.

No other world religion besides Christianity presents a god of grace, let alone the concept of grace. Every other religion bases a person's acceptance on his or her works and merit. Christianity stands alone in saving men and women by God's grace and on the merits of God's only begotten Son. Therefore no other religion can guarantee salvation, victory, or heaven to anyone, because no one on earth can be confident in his or her goodness, merit, or works. The Bible clearly and rightfully states that "all have sinned and fall short of the glory of God" (Romans 3:23). Only Jesus met the perfect standard of God's glory. By dying for our sins, He offers to us the perfection He alone possesses. Only those who rely on God's grace can be confident in this present life and in the future.

I will never forget the day I was reprimanding my youngest son, Braden, for bad behavior. He was only five years old, and in our family he was famous for inventing his own version of Scripture. On this occasion he tried to justify his actions by asking, "Doesn't the Bible say 'Thou shalt not blame the one that did it'?" I was just about to correct his theology when he spoke out with, "Stop! Stop! I know what the Bible says. It says all sin makes you short, and that's why I'm still so much shorter than my brother."

Though I got a hearty laugh out of his misguided notion, it was important to set the record straight! Understanding that my little guy was under the tremendous condemnation of guilt, I explained to him that everyone gets it wrong and everyone must pay for his own sins. In other words, the one who did it will be blamed. I further explained that because we're all to blame and have fallen short, God sent Jesus to meet the perfect standard and pay for our wrongdoings so we can have access to God. Braden seemed quite relieved that day. He not only escaped punishment, but he got a great lecture on grace!

What was true for my youngest son is true for us. The only way we can escape the blame for the wrong we've done is through the grace of God available in Christ Jesus. And that is exactly what we have received through Christ. John 1:17 says, "The law was given through Moses, but grace and truth came through Jesus Christ." Truth tells us of our guilt and our deficit because of sin. Then grace comes, covers the deficit sin has left us with, and makes us right with God. From this fullness of grace, we can then draw on even more grace, or as John 1:16 declares, "Of His fullness we have all received, and grace for grace."

The Battle Is On

The battle for grace is real. The outcome of this battle is crucial to your spiritual well-being, mental health, physical health, emotional health, and social well-being. Grace affects every area of your life!

Without grace you will live in constant condemnation and always find yourself outside the threshold of grace. You'll live without the power of the Lord to overcome the difficulties and trials of life.

Without grace you'll live in fear and constant anxiety. You'll be perpetually burdened under the intimidating lies and threats that swirl around you. You'll never know the supreme power of grace that gives you boldness to enter the divine supply room.

Without grace you'll measure every endeavor by your physical stamina and health. This will limit you to do only what you feel capable of. You'll miss glorious opportunities and the chance to experience the abundant life Jesus promised.

Bishop Phillip Brooks, who wrote the lyrics to "O Little Town of Bethlehem," once wrote,

> Do not pray for easy lives. Pray to be stronger men.
> Do not pray for tasks equal to your powers. Pray for
> powers equal to your tasks. Then the doing of your
> work shall be no miracle, but you shall be the miracle.

God's grace takes us beyond the range of our humanity into the realms of what He alone can accomplish. He makes us His miracle of grace!

Without grace you will never reach full emotional health. You'll be constantly plucking the petals of the proverbial daisy, saying, "He loves me; He loves me not." You will never realize the confident boldness of knowing Jesus's love, and therefore you'll never be able to fully communicate or manifest that grace to others.

Without the divine supply of grace, you'll never have healthy relationships with others. You'll hold others to unrealistic expectations, be impatient with their shortcomings, and continually be writing people out of your life.

To have and live by the grace of God, you'll need to battle to keep the roads clear to the ammunition supply of grace. Even now, whether or not you're cognizant of it, you're battling. I've learned that, every day, I'm battling forces beyond me. To win the battle of life, I need the surpluses of grace. Like me, you're daily battling for grace every time you

- endeavor to overcome your difficulties.
- desire to improve your attitude.
- seek to be kind to others.
- choose to believe the Word of God.
- look beyond yourself to God.
- attempt to overcome your weaknesses.

The victory over our difficulties and attitudes—to gain the ability to be kind, to maintain spiritual faith, and to be strong—only comes by God's grace. The good news is that you can have all the grace you require to help in your time of need. Grace is ready, available, and totally accessible in the throne room of grace. This powerhouse of glory is waiting for you. It's worth fighting every obstacle and hindrance that stands in your way.

What is our battle? Our battle is to get to the throne room of grace and keep the troops supplied with the ammunition of grace that wins the victory over the giants and deficits in life. It's a constant battle to obtain grace, rely on grace, hold grace, maintain grace, and live by the power of God's grace. Unless we receive daily supplies, we'll never be able to win the battle for grace!

Dear Lord, here I am before Your throne of grace. I have entered boldly, not by my own merits but because of everything Jesus Christ has done for me. I come in His name and present my need of grace to You. I thank You for the overcoming power of Your grace. I thank You for the access I have to this divine supply. Help me come often to this grand room of grace. Help me ask again and again, without embarrassment, for this glorious provision. Never let me leave Your presence without armloads of grace to help in my time of need. Because of Jesus! Amen.

For consideration:

1. What lies or intimidations have kept you from boldly entering the throne room of grace?

2. What does it mean to you personally to know you're appearing before a throne of grace?

3. How would you describe your "time of need"?

4. Review and comment on these words and phrases from Hebrews 4:16:

   - let us
   - come
   - boldly
   - obtain mercy
   - find grace
   - help

5. How would you characterize the battle for grace?

Four

The Enemies of Grace

We do not wrestle against flesh and blood, but against principalities,
against powers, against the rulers of the darkness of this age,
against spiritual hosts of wickedness in the heavenly places.

EPHESIANS 6:12

During the Civil War in the United States, both the North and South employed the services of spies. These spies were extremely difficult for either side to detect because the people on both sides spoke the same language, shared nearly the same culture, and had no exceptionally unique physical features.

Some of the most successful spies during this conflict were women. Unlike men, women were less likely to fall under suspicion. While caring for household duties, they listened to conversations held by military personnel and then relayed the information to couriers, who delivered it to command posts.

During this time of national conflict, Rose O'Neal Greenhow was a widow of high social standing living in Washington D.C.—and one of the most notorious of the Confederate spies. Though her sympathies for the Confederate cause were well known, she was considered above suspicion because of how obvious her Southern affections were. Besides this fact, Mrs. Greenhow held one of the most hallowed vocations in life—she was the mother of four children.

Rose held a variety of soirees, where she entertained generals and commanders in the Union army. She not only listened in on conversations, but she asked questions about specific military maneuvers and then feigned ignorance and annoyance toward any talk of war. Using her feminine wiles, she gathered important information for the Southern forces.

It took a long time for the Union army to suspect Rose of any misconduct. However, once she fell under suspicion, federal detectives followed and tracked her every move. They observed her in the act of gathering and forwarding military secrets to Confederate agents. Until Mrs. Greenhow was identified, arrested, and imprisoned, the Union was losing key battles. Her exposure was one of the most monumental turning points in the Civil War,[1] because soon after her exile to the South, the North again had the advantage and eventually won the war.

Just as it was difficult for the Northern forces to recognize and identify the matron of Washington society as a dangerous spy, it's often hard to recognize and identify the opponents of grace. However, until we do, we're in jeopardy of losing key battles for grace.

We have real enemies that want to keep us from the power source of grace. These enemies know that without God's grace, we are easily defeated. Even the things I love to do become tedious, overwhelming duties when I'm living without utilizing the grace of God. I've learned that to avoid the "Nebuchadnezzar Syndrome," I need to take daily trips to the throne room of God. There I receive the grace I desperately need to be a wife, mother, grandmother, friend, example, and witness for Jesus to this dying world.

Honestly, I've come to rely on the grace of Jesus for everything I do. Even cooking dinner will send me running to the throne of grace for creativity, energy, skill, blessing, and time management. Do you know what? I find it there! God blesses and has blessed my kitchen in extraordinary ways when I've first gone to His throne room.

Remember, the Enemy has one goal—to keep you from the throne of grace. To achieve this goal, he will use all sorts of tactics, including intimidation, insecurities, conceit, condemnation, distraction, and lies.

So in the battle of grace, it's imperative that (1) we recognize we have an enemy, (2) we understand that any enemy's objective is to keep us from accessing and utilizing the divine supply of grace, (3) we know who all the enemies are, and (4) we have an awareness of their tactics. The enemy is not easily recognizable and often poses as a comrade.

You

The first enemy to grace is easily recognizable. You've seen her a million times. You've observed her since she was a child. Every time you look in the mirror, you get a good look at her. That's right! You are your own enemy—your own *worst* enemy!

How so? Chances are you're harder on yourself than anyone else is. You put expectations on yourself, your strength, your mind, your heart, your life, and your relationships, and these expectations are more exacting than anyone else's. That's why you take it so hard when you fail. As a pastor's wife who has talked, ministered, and prayed with many women, I know self is the number-one enemy women battle against, yet we rarely recognize this enemy as a foe rather than friend. When I talk to these precious women, I always pray grace over their lives. Then I exhort them, "Will you please have some grace for yourself?"

One of the young women I frequently have the pleasure of ministering to was attracted to a certain young man she worked with. She prayed and prayed that God would remove her attraction to him. She berated herself. She barred herself from seeing him. She dismissed every thought of him. She made rules about the distance she should keep from him. She even breathed a sigh of relief when he moved out of state. But you know what? That very man wrote her a letter confessing his attraction to her. He said he'd been praying for her ever since they worked together. He asked if she would ever consider marrying him. She wrote back an emphatic yes!

Today they are happily married with two young sons. My friend almost cut herself off from grace. Rather than running into the throne room of grace, she condemned herself, rebuked her desire, made rules for herself, and put stringent restrictions on herself. These self-imposed sanctions almost scared off the man of her dreams. But thank God, His grace prevailed!

Here's a ten-question test to prove your enemy status to yourself:

1. What is your response when you get things wrong? (How easy is it for you to admit you got it wrong? If it's easy, then you're growing in grace. If you struggle to simply admit you're capable of getting things wrong at times, however, you have a grace issue.)

2. How many items would you put on your self-improvement list? (More than ten readily puts you in the self-enmity category.)

3. How do you feel when you put your foot in your mouth? (Do you just want to die? Do you want to hide from those people who heard you? Do you make incessant apologies and try to explain again and again what you were really trying to communicate?)

4. What do you tell yourself about you? (Is it positive or negative? Do you continually think about what you've gotten wrong and get wrong? What's the tone of the sermons you preach to yourself?)

5. How would you rate your level of self-condemnation? (Do you blame yourself for everything that goes wrong in your life? Do you say things to yourself like, *If you hadn't said this* or *If you hadn't done that?* Are you constantly questioning your motives?)

6. Do you often feel scared to move forward? (Are you overly aware of your past failures? Do you tend to dwell on your weaknesses? Do you try to do only what you're good at, experienced at, or are comfortable with? Do new things throw you off balance?)

7. How much sway do the opinions of other people about you have on the decisions you make? (Do you change your activities, ways of doing things, or places you go because you know certain people disapprove? Do you suppress your true feelings? Are you afraid to be honest around your peers?)

8. Do you berate yourself over your failures, weaknesses, lapses, and infractions? (Are you often surprised by your failure? Do you ask yourself, *How could I possibly do that?* Or do you say to yourself, *I don't know what came over me!* or *That's so unlike me?* Do you feel the need to talk about your failure over and over with other people to try to understand yourself or make yourself feel less guilty?)

9. Do you feel the constant need to say you're sorry to others and to constantly justify what you said, did, or

desire to do? (Do you analyze past conversations and events? Do you feel the need to rehearse and play certain words, scenes, and actions again and again in your mind? Do you bring up past conversations with friends and feel the need to qualify certain words or actions again and again?)

10. Do you allow past failure to disqualify you from present opportunities? (Do you suffer from feelings of unworthiness? Are you dealing with insecurities that threaten to erode your confidence in the love of Jesus for you? Do you struggle with the reality that Jesus loves you?)

The answers to these questions determine at what level you're lacking in grace. If you use these questions to condemn yourself further, then you're missing the whole point. The real issue is that you need grace, and you have to fight your own self-evaluation to get to the throne room of grace for your supply!

During my first year of college, I lived in a dormitory filled with beautiful girls. Like most young women away from home for the first time, I was burdened with insecurities. I often tried to assuage those insecurities by eating. I gained so much weight that I couldn't fit into my clothes. Of course, I blamed myself for my voracious appetite. The more I ate, the more I blamed myself. The more I blamed myself, the more I ate! It was a vicious cycle.

Determined to lose weight, I wrote out every Scripture I could find about overeating. To tell you the truth, the Bible doesn't have many options, but that didn't stop me from pulling whatever verses I could out of context and pasting them to the wall of my dormitory room.

Glaring at me from one wall was Proverbs 23:2 from the King

James Version: "Put a knife to thy throat, if thou be a man given to appetite." I preferred the King James Version for these verses because they seemed more judicial. Another wall ornament declared, "Be not desirous of his dainties: for they are deceitful meat" (Proverbs 23:3 KJV). Every wall, and even the back of the door, bore one of my handwritten placards. Not one of them kept me from overeating. Not one! Their effect was just the opposite. I felt even more condemned and absolutely helpless against my own appetite.

Today this story reminds me of Paul's warning to the Colossians: "These things indeed have an appearance of wisdom in self-imposed religion, false humility, and neglect of the body, but are of no value against the indulgence of the flesh" (Colossians 2:23). That was a lesson I learned firsthand. Not one of my self-imposed sanctions, self-efforts, or threats gave me power to resist my appetite or release me from the self-loathing I felt when I failed.

My reaction to my failure was more self-berating and more stringent restrictions, which led to less and less grace. My own failed attempts kept me from crying out for the very grace I needed to help in my time of need. I thought I had to hate food, refuse any sugary indulgence, and lose weight to enter the throne room of God.

This was not God's disposition toward me. He saw me and observed my constant condemnation, and He was constantly calling me into His grace. It took a full year of dismal failure before I threw myself before His throne.

Looking back, I can clearly identify the enemy who kept me from grace—me. In my self-effort to perfect myself, I had almost ruined myself. All of us must fight a daily battle against ourselves for grace. Let me be clear on this. No self-effort, no self-berating, no self-imposed restrictions, no self-made sanctions will give you a better attitude, a better perspective, a better self-image, a better heart, a better appetite, a better lifestyle, or better strength. What you need is God's grace! Your notions and stubborn desire to get yourself right, however, will keep you from the very grace that will transform you and make a better you.

After teaching the women's Bible study at church one Friday morning and then walking toward the back door, I saw a woman I knew sobbing. She reached out her hand and asked if I had a moment to talk. I sat down, and she told me how she felt responsible for plunging her husband into debt. It had to do with the remodeling of a room in their house. She thought both some of her decisions and her indecision had resulted in extra expense. She was beside herself with guilt, blame, and condemnation.

As I listened to her saga, one thought ran through my mind: This precious daughter of the Almighty God needed grace. She needed God's grace to forgive herself. She needed God's grace to have the wisdom to get the job done. She needed God's grace to keep going forward. You can imagine how I prayed for her! It was as if I grabbed her hand and dragged her into the throne room of grace. I prayed grace all over her heart, mind, and body. I prayed grace over her from the top of her head to the soles of her feet! When I said, "Amen," I looked up and saw that her countenance had visibly lifted! Just think, where would she have been if I hadn't rushed her into the throne room of grace?

Don't let "you" keep you out of the throne room of grace! The worse you feel about yourself, the more you need to get in there and receive His divine grace. We all get it wrong more often than we get it right. Life is hard, and perfect people don't exist. We all need grace!

Pride

Pride is another aspect of self, but I'm putting it in its own category. Although pride can be an overcompensation for insecurity, more times than not it's an overinflated view of ourselves. Three times the Bible states that God resists the proud but gives grace to the humble (Proverbs 3:34; James 4:6; 1 Peter 5:5). Pride keeps us from the throne room of grace because pride is the attitude that says *I can do it without God* or *I'll do it for God*. At three years old, my youngest grandson used to love to thump his chest and announce loudly, "I can do it myself!" This usually came at inconvenient times, like when I was trying to grab his hand to take him across the street, navigating him through a crowd, or attempting to strap him into his car seat quickly. His pride never made my job as a grandma easy.

That's exactly how we are at times. Without intending to, we incorporate pride into our daily tasks. Whenever I think I'm going to do something for God rather than by or with God, I'm in the area of pride. Remember my Nebuchadnezzar experience? Well, one thing I specifically remember from that day is all the things I thought *I* had done for God. I hadn't asked for or felt His enabling power. I had ventured off on my own, and I certainly felt pride in my accomplishments—that is, until it all began to fall apart.

God doesn't want us doing anything without His grace. He wants to bring His presence and infusion to all our activities. God is relational. In the Bible, He presents Himself as Father, Friend, Savior, and Shepherd. These are relational terms. God wants our fellowship. He wants our attention. He wants to work with us, through us, and in us.

God is repulsed by our pride because it puts distance between Him and us. Pride neglects and ignores God. He resists the proud. He keeps His distance from those who distance themselves from Him. However, James 4:8 tells us that if we draw near to God, He will draw near to us. Pride puts us at a distance, but humility will draw us close to God.

Though the proud person is still dependent on God for the necessities of life—the beat of his heart, the breath in his lungs, life, sunshine, rain, food, and other life basics—he goes about his life ignoring God and never asking for His presence and help. Don't think this is limited to non-believers. No! We all have times when we get a little overly confident in our own abilities. Sometimes we're simply hyper-focused on our goal, and pride sneaks in the door and distracts us from the throne room of grace.

One Gospel story that never ceases to convict me is found in Luke 7. Jesus had been invited into the home of Simon the Pharisee. When Jesus arrived, however, Simon virtually ignored Him. He didn't extend to Jesus even the most common courtesies of the culture. He didn't wash Jesus's feet. He didn't greet Him with a kiss. He didn't anoint Him with the fragrance of his house.

Another guest arrived in Simon's house—a woman notorious for her sin. Seeing Jesus, she ran to Him and fell at His feet. She drew the attention of the whole house to Him. She wept loudly over Him. She poured perfume on His feet and began to kiss them and wipe them with her hair. She literally humiliated herself before Jesus. You can imagine Simon's dismay! In his heart he was thinking that if Jesus were truly a prophet, He would have never allowed such a spectacle. After all, this woman was a sinner.

Then Jesus called Simon out by asking him a question in the form of a parable. The parable concerned two debtors. One owed a great debt and the other a minor debt. The benefactor forgave both debts. Jesus then asked Simon who loved the benefactor more.

Simon answered correctly when he said the one who was forgiven the greater debt would be more appreciative. Then Jesus identified Simon's debt. Simon had not shown the least of courtesies to Jesus, yet the woman, "who was a sinner" (verse 37), extended all the Eastern hospitality Simon had omitted.

I find myself in this parable again and again. No, I'm not the notorious woman. I'm more like Simon. I've invited Jesus into my heart and life, but because of pride I've often left Him alone and neglected on my premises. I do this because I forget I've been forgiven a great debt. Unlike the notorious woman, I'm unaware of my great need for Jesus.

This woman experienced the grace of Jesus. She was forgiven of all her sins. The result was that she made a spectacle of Jesus. He couldn't be ignored in her life, all because she recognized her need for grace.

Unfortunately, I think I can do quite a bit in my own strength without the added blessing of grace in my life. It often takes a "notorious woman," someone making a spectacle of Jesus, or even Jesus publicly calling me out, before I realize my pride has kept me from the throne room of grace.

Pride gets everything in our life out of whack. It keeps us from the throne room of grace, it puts distance between God and us, and it robs us of every iota of grace we have. Those in the grip of pride look down on others and feel superior.

It's interesting how much prideful people expect of others and how little they expect of themselves. Their attitudes of entitlement make them feel that others should make up for the deficits they experience. In looking to others, they miss the divine opportunity to receive the grace of God. Instead they tend to live in a world of blame, bitterness, and bruised egos. It's a fact that people, even with the best intentions, will let us down, so the prideful person will live with perpetual disappointment.

God reserves His grace for the humble. The person who realizes how desperately he or she needs the grace of God is the person who receives the grace of God.

A friend of mine was going through a tremendous trial. She was extremely weak, overly burdened, and humiliated by what she was experiencing. She asked for prayer. I replied that I was excited to pray for her because we were guaranteed the grace of God. I told her God said in His Word that He would not resist a contrite heart (Psalm 34:18). He is drawn to our broken spirit. Furthermore, Jesus promised that those who are poor in spirit are truly blessed and have access to the storehouses of heaven (Matthew 5:3). We prayed, and God's grace was evident in her life and situation almost immediately.

The wisest thing we can do is admit our deficits and inadequacies before God. Peter, after declaring that God resists the proud and gives grace to the humble, included this exhortation: "Therefore humble yourselves under the mighty hand of God, that He may exalt you in due time" (1 Peter 5:6). When we recognize our limitations and take those limitations to the throne room of God, we're acting in humility. Our boldness in entering is not because of our qualifications, self-effort, or righteousness—that would be conceit. No, we enter because of the accomplishments, good work, and righteousness of Jesus. The Bible says our best is like filthy rags before God (Isaiah 64:6). We must constantly battle against the pride in us that resists His help.

The Law

Here is another enemy masquerading as a friend. It's the law, and it's not our friend. The law is our condemnation. It sets before us an impossible standard, one we all have fallen short of. The law offers us no help, strength, or power to meet its demands. The law has no mercy and condemns us without emotion. The law is the law!

This condemnation increases when we realize the law is not just the Ten Commandments. No, it's deeper, wider, and more incriminating than we can imagine. Generations ago, people measured themselves by their ability to adhere to the Ten Commandments. That idea was jettisoned as more and more people recognized their inability to keep just ten simple commands. However, those Ten

Commandments are more demanding than anyone realized until Jesus preached the Sermon on the Mount.

There Jesus brought to bear the full implications of the law. The commandments didn't simply govern our activity; they were meant to order our thoughts. Suddenly the command to not commit murder was not just about physically taking a life, but included contemplating murder in our minds. Hateful, vindictive thoughts and evil intentions were the precursors to murder, and the one who entertained such thoughts was guilty of murder.

With the same magnitude, adultery was not just about a physical act of sex with someone other than your spouse. Adultery was a heart issue. If you thought about sex with someone you weren't married to or if you entertained lustful fantasies, you had already committed adultery in your heart. Ugh!

Jesus brought a greater application to the Ten Commandments than anyone had ever realized. Suddenly those ten simple commandments were impossibilities, and all mankind was guilty according to those commands!

Jesus didn't come to do away with the law, but to fulfill it, and He did so with His own life. "'Do not think that I came to destroy the Law or the Prophets. I did not come to destroy but to fulfill'" (Matthew 5:17), He said. Jesus came and did what no one had done before Him or has since. Jesus perfectly met even the most stringent requirements of the law with complete righteousness.

As we stated before and will state again and again, Jesus lived the life you could not live but should have lived. Your own life condemned you, but Jesus's perfect obedience and life have brought you grace.

Are you living your life under the law? Perhaps the Ten Commandments don't govern your life and condemn you, but your own set of shoulds and should nots do.

We all tend to have an unwritten law for ourselves, and we judge ourselves by this law. When we have good days, we feel welcomed to enter the throne room of grace. On our bad days, however, we slink away from even the presence of God, and like Adam and Eve, we hide "naked" among the trees (Genesis 3:7-8).

Here is another grace test. Do you feel you should

1. be kinder to others?
2. react slower?
3. be more patient?
4. eat healthier by going
    • non-gluten?
    • caffeine free?
    • sugar free?
    • vegan?
    • vegetarian?
    • dairy free?
    • nut free?
    • food free?
5. be more physically fit?
6. read more nonfiction?
7. learn another language?
8. put more effort into certain areas of your life, like
    • friendships?
    • cooking?
    • cleaning?
    • decorating?

9. go to church more?

10. budget your money better?

11. put more into your savings account?

12. be more responsible fiscally?

13. take better care of your possessions?

14. be more responsible?

15. be better organized?

16. pray more?

17. read your Bible more?

18. tithe more?

Or do you feel you should *not*

1. say anything unkind?

2. be quick to get angry?

3. eat sugary treats?

4. indulge yourself?

5. eat cheesy, greasy, loaded nachos (oops that's mine)?

6. be impatient?

7. worry?

8. talk so much?

9. be afraid?

10. divulge so much information?

11. use your credit card?

12. spend money?

13. waste time?

You might be living under the tyranny of your own law. Its

power, like the Ten Commandments, is only to condemn you and showcase all your imperfections. The shoulds and should nots don't offer you any help against the indulgences of your flesh. Rather, they infiltrate your thoughts, constantly assail you, and rob you of your joy. Your own law is an enemy to grace.

You must battle against your own standards to make your way daily to the throne room of grace. Remember, these self-imposed standards want to substitute for, sabotage, and steal God's grace from your life. They have the appearance of righteousness and goodness, but they offer no help to improve your life. When you feel the pressure of rules, regulations, and self-imposed sanctions bearing down on you, run—don't walk—to the throne room of God!

The World

I try to wear my most beat-up clothes when I'm in my creative cooking mood because I usually splash myself. I don't look pretty. Amid this chaos of creativity, however, I often realize I'm lacking a key ingredient. That's when I seriously hate going to the market, but I slip on my flip-flops, grab my purse and keys, and off I go.

At the checkout stand, I'm barraged with the images of perfect women. No, the women are not behind me in line or even in front of me. They surround me on the covers of many of the magazines. They're beautiful. Their hair is perfection. They look like they've never suffered with lipstick on their teeth or mascara settling in the lines beneath their eyes. Their figures have no unwanted bulges or bumps. They have no lines or wrinkles. They are perpetually young. They're wearing the current style in perfect order. In utter contrast to me, they testify to what a real woman should look like.

As if these alluring images were not censuring enough, the other magazines highlight beautiful homes with perfect gardens.

Brilliantly organized and spotless kitchens shine in stark contrast to the flour-spotted kitchen I left in absolute disarray.

These magazine covers feature articles on how to be more tantalizing to your spouse or boyfriend. Another article suggests a diet to lose 20 pounds in 20 days, with another article below it for the most scrumptious chocolate cake ever! Every periodical contains several how-to articles. They offer more rules, regulations, and rituals with the promise that if I strictly follow and adhere to them, my life will be greatly enhanced.

Nonsense! No one can live up to the images our culture is constantly giving us. No one! Every day the media seems to uncover some model or actress's secret addiction, problem, or heartache. The lives they've shown to the public have been mere images, full of make-believe.

I recently read an article about one particularly beautiful actress who has successfully played many roles. During a question-and-answer time, a young woman asked her a probing question: "After playing so many different roles, do you know who you really are?" Tears began to pour down the actress's face, and she seemed stunned by the question. She shook her head no, and in a soft whisper said, "I'm not sure." This actress couldn't live up to the images she portrayed. Her genuine personality was lost, shuffled, even discarded among the many roles she assumed.

The world will give you images that are simply that—images. These images appear on the screen, on magazine covers, and on billboards. But like the gods of old described in Psalm 115:5-8 (KJV), "They have mouths, but they do not speak; eyes they have, but they do not see; they have ears, but they do not hear; noses they have, but they do not smell; they have hands, but they do not handle; feet they have, but they do not walk; nor do they mutter through their throat. Those who make them are like them; so is everyone who trusts in them." These images can't help us be better versions of ourselves.

The culture presents unreal images to its constituents. It demands that they live up to these demi-gods. The images are intimidating, but they're not real. The most revered in society can't even live up to the idols they've created.

When we try to be like and live up to the standards of the images we see, we're bound to fail. In truth, everyone ages. Everyone gets lined and wrinkled. Hair naturally turns gray. Houses get dusty. Furniture and clothes go out of style. People gain weight. Body shapes change. Age weakens everyone. Viruses infect everybody. Such is real life!

The world doesn't offer you any grace. It presents an unreachable standard and then taunts the one who tries to attain it. The media is notorious for praising someone's rise to stardom, cheering their self-destructive ways, and then condemning their demise. Culture offers slogans and philosophies that don't work:

The power is within you.

If it feels good, do it.

If you feel it, then it's right for you.

You'll never know until you try.

Fulfillment comes by indulging every desire.

These slogans, if followed, ultimately lead to self-destruction, addiction, and frustration. They keep you from the very storehouse of grace that will save you, free you, and quench the deep spiritual thirst within you.

Satan

No doubt you were expecting this next enemy—Satan. Satan is the absolute enemy of grace. In Revelation 12:10 he's called "the accuser of our brethren." His constant preoccupation is informing God how each one of His creations and subjects falls short, fails, and deserves condemnation. One of his many titles is *devil*, which means slanderer. This refers to just one of the many methods he employs to keep Christians from the throne room of grace.

The devil constantly assails you with doubts, threats, condemning thoughts, reminders of your shortcomings, your past sins, and your failures to keep you from the surplus of grace. He knows spiritual power awaits you in God's throne room, and he does his best to keep you from going through the door. He knows God's divine arsenal of grace will equip you for victory, and victory is not what Satan wants you to have or walk in.

The apostle Peter was well aware of the tactics of the devil. In one of his last conversations with Jesus before His crucifixion, Jesus warned him of Satan's intentions. "'Simon, Simon! Indeed, Satan has asked for you, that he may sift you like wheat. But I have prayed for you, that your faith should not fail; and when you have returned to Me, strengthen your brethren'" (Luke 22:31-32).

Peter indeed went through a sifting. He fell asleep in the garden of Gethsemane after Jesus asked him to watch and pray. He foolishly lashed out with a sword when the soldiers came with Judas to arrest Jesus. He warmed himself next to the fire kindled by the enemies of Jesus. He denied that he knew Jesus to a maiden who opened the gate to the high priest's courtyard. His second denial occurred when he dismissed his relationship to Jesus to another young woman. His final denial, before the rooster heralded the dawn of the day, was when he denounced Jesus with oaths to one of the soldiers of the high priest (Luke 22:45-46,54-62; John 18:10).

Peter knew firsthand the strength of the Enemy's tactics. Peter had not only failed himself and his own resolves, but he had fallen prey to Satan's intimidation and denied the Lord of glory. So with firsthand experience, Peter warned, "Be sober, be vigilant; because your adversary the devil walks about like a roaring lion, seeking whom he may devour. Resist him, steadfast in the faith, knowing that the same sufferings are experienced by your brotherhood in the world. But may the God of all grace, who called us to His eternal glory by Christ Jesus, after you have suffered a while, perfect, establish, strengthen, and settle you" (1 Peter 5:8-10).

Peter, having fallen prey to the devil, knew his enemy. Having once succumbed, he was wise to his tactics and able to warn other believers.

Satan knows what we, too, often fail to realize—the infinite power of God's grace toward us. Jesus's powerful grace delivered us out of the hand of Satan. His grace washed away past condemnation. His grace dressed us in robes of righteousness. His grace gave us a heavenly position. His grace fortifies us with every spiritual blessing in Christ Jesus. His grace supplies us with all the power we need for victory over every device of the Enemy. Is it any wonder that we must battle for grace?

Know Your Enemies

Identifying your enemies, understanding their tactics, and knowing their end game is of the utmost importance. Your enemies are you, pride, the law, the world, and the devil. You're never safe alone in their company. They employ lies, intimidation, and condemnation to endeavor to block and impede your passage to and into the throne room of grace. Daily you must fight against these foes and make your way to the throne room of grace so you can be fully equipped for victory!

....

Dear Lord, I realize that I, myself, have been an enemy of grace. I have sought to live in my own righteousness. I have attempted to attain righteousness by self-imposed sanctions, rules, and rituals that have not improved my standing before You. I ask Your forgiveness for my enmity toward grace. Help me recognize the forces that impose themselves against Your grace. Keep me from any attempts to live under the law rather than in the throne room of grace. Help me to shut out all the intimidating voices of the law, the culture, and the devil. When they seem to bar the entrance to grace, help me not to pull back in fear, but to charge forward in boldness into Your holy room. Thank You for Your great love, victory, and the grace You have waiting for me. Because of the grace that is mine in Christ Jesus, I pray. Amen!

For consideration:

1. List some of your self-imposed rules.

2. What do you find surprising about the identity of the enemies of grace? What foes did you expect to read about?

3. Write about a time when your own laws kept you from grace.

4. What frustrations have you felt in trying to keep your own law?

5. In what way have you felt the condemnation of the law?

6. List some of the unreal expectations our culture places on women.

7. List three areas where you've felt the intimidation of the Enemy.

8. How would you describe the battle for grace?

9. As you review Hebrews 4:16, what discoveries are you making concerning God's throne of grace?

Five

Qualified by Grace

*I have written to you briefly, exhorting and testifying
that this is the true grace in which you stand.*

1 Peter 5:12

Billy Sunday was only a newborn when his father died. His mother, unable to cope with raising Billy and his brother, relinquished custody of her sons to an orphanage when Billy was 13 years old. At 15 he ran away from the orphanage and ended up in Nevada, Iowa. There he was taken under the wing of Colonel John Scott, who hired and housed the teen and sent him back to school. In school, Billy excelled at baseball. He was a fast runner and outshone the other boys with his ability to retrieve the ball and fire it to the various bases with lightning speed.

At one of his games, he was spotted and recruited by Cap Anson, who managed the Chicago White Stockings. Billy dropped out of high school, moved to Chicago, and began his baseball career in 1883. By his own testimony, he was a hardened young man. He gambled hard, played hard, and lived hard. Monday through Friday he practiced baseball with his team. On Saturday he played ball, and on Sunday he went to the saloon with his teammates. Billy only occasionally indulged as the other players drank themselves into a stupor, but he was constantly in their company.

On one of those ominous Sundays, Billy left the bar "tanked up" and walked to one of the street corners in Chicago. Across the street, accompanied by singers, a band played hymns on trombones, trumpets, and flutes. Someone invited Billy to follow the band to the Pacific Garden Mission. There Billy heard the gospel of grace and surrendered his life to Jesus Christ.

Billy played professional baseball for the Chicago White Stockings until he transferred to the Pittsburgh Alleghenies, finally ending up with the Philadelphia Phillies. In 1891 Billy was offered a lucrative contract of $3500 a year to return to the Chicago White Stockings. He deferred their offer to evangelize and counsel young men at the Chicago YMCA for $83 a month.

In 1893 J. Wilbur Chapman asked Billy to assist him as a co-evangelist. Billy worked with Chapman for three years, until he struck out on his own in 1896. Billy Sunday became one of the most famous evangelists of the twentieth century. His sermons were colorful, impassioned, and full of colloquialisms. In many of his sermons, he highlighted the marvels of God's grace toward him. Billy testified about being a gambler, a drinker, and a brawler before he met Christ. One of his most famous lines was his own paraphrase of Hebrews 7:25: "Therefore He is also able to save to the uttermost those who come to God through Him, since He always lives to make intercession for them." Billy liked to say God saved him from the "guttermost."

Think about it for a moment. What power could transform a young, hardened orphan, runaway, gambler, and professional baseball player into an evangelist for the cause of Christ? Grace!

Grace drew Billy to God. Grace forgave Billy's sins. Grace

cleansed Billy from the stains of his past. Grace qualified Billy to become a servant of God.

God's grace not only reaches to the depths of human depravity and calls men and women to salvation; it also forgives, cleanses, and qualifies all those who come to Jesus by faith! It calls to the "guttermost" and saves to the "uttermost," all by and through the grace of God!

The Generosity of Grace

> It is of faith that it might be according to grace, so that the promise might be sure to all the seed, not only to those who are of the law, but also to those who are of the faith of Abraham, who is the father of us all (Romans 4:16).

Grace is offered to sinners and saints alike, indiscriminate of social status, background, heritage, success, wealth, education, or talent. Grace offers the gifts of Jesus Christ to all who will believe by faith. Anyone who believes in the great qualifying work of Jesus, the Messiah, can be forgiven, cleansed, called, and used by God in His service!

When I was 12 I signed up to sing in the choir for the community's Easter Sunrise Service. Placed as a second soprano, I joined my voice with the others singing the hymn "Wonderful Grace of Jesus." I was so taken with the pure joy of singing the upbeat melody that I almost missed the glory of the lyrics I was proclaiming. As I practiced the song one day in the car, my dad joined in. As we sang together with gusto, the full force of the words began to sink in.

> Wonderful Grace of Jesus, greater than all my sin;
> How shall my tongue describe it,

Where shall its praise begin?
Taking away my burden, setting my spirit free;
For the Wonderful Grace of Jesus reaches me!

Refrain

Wonderful the matchless Grace of Jesus,
Deeper than the mighty rolling sea;
Wonderful Grace, all sufficient for me, for even me.
Broader than the scope of my transgressions,
Greater far than all my sin and shame
O magnify the precious name of Jesus,
Praise His Name!

Wonderful Grace of Jesus, reaching to all the lost;
By it I have been pardoned, saved to the uttermost
Chains have been torn asunder,
Giving me liberty;
And the wonderful grace of Jesus reaches me.

Wonderful Grace of Jesus, reaching the most defiled,
By its transforming power,
Making me God's dear child,
Purchasing peace and Heaven, for all eternity;
And the Wonderful Grace of Jesus reaches me.

Grace is God's way of saving us, forgiving us, cleansing us, and transforming us so we can be qualified to be His instruments of grace! And grace is wonderful because it calls to everyone. Jesus said, "'Many are called, but few are chosen'" (Matthew 22:14). God's call goes out to all.

Jesus illustrated God's great call by telling a parable, found in

Matthew 22:1-14. In the story, a king invites all his friends and the nobility to his son's lavish wedding. For various reasons, those invited refused to come. Some made light of the invitation. Others didn't want to take time away from their businesses and farms to attend. Still others resented the invitation and abused those who invited them. The father was furious with the response, and he instructed his servants to go into the highways and invite anyone they found to the wedding.

The servants obeyed and gathered both the bad and good until the wedding hall was filled with people. The king came into the assembly to greet the guests. Among those in attendance was a man without a wedding garment; he had not changed his clothes into the proper attire provided. The man had no excuse for his behavior. The king was enraged and had the man thrown out.

Jesus was communicating the gracious generosity of God's call. It goes to the highways of life and invites both the good and bad to come, be forgiven, exchange their old garments for beautiful ones, and enjoy the bounty of His goodness.

Those who respond to God's call cannot, however, remain in their old garments. Grace redresses us in the garments of Jesus's righteousness. By its very nature, grace changes us so that we are equipped and qualified to be guests in God's great kingdom and partake of His goodness.

Grace isn't for the worthy but for the unworthy. Grace qualifies those who could never qualify themselves. Grace did for Billy Sunday what Billy could never do for himself. Grace met Billy Sunday right where he was, on a street corner in Chicago. Grace wooed him just as he was, a sinner, and brought him to salvation. Grace offered Billy Sunday forgiveness of sins through Jesus Christ. When he believed by faith in Jesus, God's grace forgave Billy, cleansed Billy, and began to transform Billy from the inside out. This drawing, forgiving, cleansing, transforming, and qualifying power of grace is wonderful indeed!

Grace—The Ultimate Transformer

The statistics concerning repeat offenders in the United States are disconcerting. Time spent in jail doesn't make a criminal into a law-abiding citizen. Half of those released from prison are back in the criminal justice system within a year. Two-thirds of those released from prison return within three years. A staggering three-quarters of all released prisoners are jailed again within five years.[1] Society has tried all sorts of different means to change these men and women, but punishment, fear of imprisonment, threats, laws, opportunities, education, and rehabilitation have failed to change at least three-quarters of all those who commit crimes. These efforts fail because they cannot change the heart.

On the other hand, grace is powerful because it goes right to the heart. Hebrews 13:9 states, "It is good that the heart be established by grace." The outward forms of punishment, education, and reward do nothing to change or establish the heart, but grace does. Grace takes hold of the heart and establishes it in Jesus. This verse explains that rules can't change us like we need to be changed. It's impossible for those things to change us, but grace, as it's established in our hearts, transforms us from the inside out.

Because grace pardons sin and gives leniency to our failures, some have wrongly concluded that grace is a license to sin. I've heard people say, "If you give people grace, you'll have a *big* problem with sin!" Jude alluded to this notion in Jude 4 when he wrote, "Certain men have crept in unnoticed, who long ago were marked out for this condemnation, ungodly men, who turn the grace of our God into lewdness and deny the only Lord God and our Lord

Jesus Christ." Notice that these men who sought to turn grace into a license to sin also denied the Lordship of Jesus!

Grace by its nature cannot be a license to sin. Why? Because the source of grace is God. He is the God of All Grace (1 Peter 5:10)! He is not the God of some grace or most grace, but of *all* grace. He's the divine source. God, by His nature, can give only good gifts. As James 1:17 states, "every good gift and every perfect gift" comes from Him. God's righteousness will not allow Him to give us anything that would cause us to sin or commit unrighteousness.

People have said to me, "Well, it doesn't matter what I do. God will forgive me because of His grace." Well, in Luke 4:12, Jesus reminded Satan that Scripture says, "You shall not tempt the LORD your God." The apostle Paul addressed this misconception of grace in Romans 6. He began the chapter with the question, "Shall we continue in sin that grace may abound?" (verse 1). He then answered this question with "Certainly not!" (verse 2)! Grace is not a license to sin. It's not permission to sin. It's just the opposite. It's the freedom, afforded by God's power, to not be dominated by sin. In Romans 6:14, Paul writes, "Sin shall not have dominion over you, for you are not under law but under grace."

Grace turns life into a classroom. Grace uses mistakes, failures, and weaknesses as opportunities for transformation. Grace takes away the terrible pressure to perform, always be perfect, and never blow it. I don't know about you, but pressure like that makes me more self-conscious and more likely to fail. Grace gives me the freedom to get it wrong and learn from my mistake.

Grace is an atmosphere so charged with constant love, patience, and mercy that you can freely admit your faults, weaknesses, and ignorance! It's only in an atmosphere of grace that we have the freedom and ability to be changed. If you stay in a place where you can't admit you've failed, you'll never learn how to get it right.

A doctor once shared with me his frustration with patients who refused to admit anything was wrong with them. He could never really help them because they wouldn't be forthcoming about where they were hurting and their symptoms. The doctor was left with no evidence to try to make a correct diagnosis. Without full disclosure, a wrong diagnosis was not only possible but probable.

Did you ever have one of those teachers in school who made you shake in your boots? I did. I remember her to this day. She demanded such perfection of her students. She was quick to ridicule any child who asked a question, missed a concept, or forgot an instruction. I was so terrified of her that I couldn't learn in her class. I had to suppress all my ignorance and put on a show of understanding just to appease her wrath. I was so nervous that I would perspire on my papers, smearing the pencil lead. It wasn't unusual to have my work returned with the word *messy* written on it in big bold red letters!

Two years later I had Mrs. Hartford. She was one of the most gracious women I have ever known. No question was ever considered stupid. In fact, she invited us to ask questions and always made the extra effort to ensure we understood the concept she was teaching. She filled the classroom with joy and creativity.

I had Mrs. Hartford in mind when I was teaching a doctrine class to young women at a Bible college. The subject of doctrine can be intimidating to students of the Bible, yet doctrine is the essential component to understanding the wondrous tenets of the Bible. We had just finished the final exam for the course, and I told the students they were going to grade their own papers. One of them, Jennifer, immediately objected.

"That's not right. What if someone isn't honest?"

I countered with, "Well, that would be their problem, not mine."

She was dissatisfied with my answer and continued to challenge me. I was resolute. "Grading your own papers is in itself a test to see how much of this class you understood, absorbed, and applied. What you got out of this class was your responsibility."

Together, as a class, we reviewed the various questions, and I offered the correct answer. One question was a bit obscure and over half the class got it wrong. I used this as an opportunity to explain the right answer in detail. I then rephrased the question, and this time the whole class knew the right answer. I said, "All right, class, I want all of you to circle the right answer for question five and cross out the wrong answer." Everyone got it right—no one got it wrong!

Immediately Jennifer, the young woman who had argued with me earlier, shot up her hand. "No! I got it wrong. Many of us got it wrong. I should have it marked wrong on my paper. That's not right."

"Jennifer," I said, "my objective is for you to know the truth. Do you know the right answer now?"

"Well, yes." She said this with hesitation.

"Then you've got it right. That's grace!" Ironically, the doctrine in question had been about grace. I thought Jennifer and the rest of the class needed just a bit more enlightenment, so I said, "God uses failure to teach us the right way."

I went on to discuss the parable of the prodigal son in Luke 15. Here was a young man who did everything wrong. He demanded his inheritance early; he abandoned his father's home; he lived a life of debauchery; he wasted all his inheritance on prodigal living and ended up eating the scraps left by unholy pigs. Yet these factors brought him "to himself" (verse 17). Only after all his failure did he begin to realize what he'd thrown away. Only then did he begin to appreciate his father's house. His failure drove him to humbly return home.

Remember the father in this parable? He was watching the road for this son who had failed so miserably. He didn't greet him with an "I told you so" lecture, a scathing rebuke, a scouring rebuff—or any punishment, for that matter. No! This father ran toward his wayward son. He fell on his neck and kissed him. He called to his servants to bring out the best robe and sandals for him, and he placed the family signet ring on his finger. He called for the fatted calf and threw a party to welcome him home (verses 20-24).

The prodigal was drawn back to his father's home because of the grace he knew was there. The grace the father showed to the son transformed him. He now knew prodigal living was wrong, and he would never go that direction again. Lesson learned.

That was the lesson I wanted to communicate to my students that day. Grace provides the best classroom for change and transformation. Grace gives us the atmosphere to get it wrong so that in the end we can get it right!

In a letter to his protégé Titus, the apostle Paul wrote, "The grace of God that brings salvation has appeared to all men, teaching us that, denying ungodliness and worldly lusts, we should live soberly, righteously, and godly in this present age" (Titus 2:11-12). That's right. God's grace teaches us. It provides the best atmosphere in the classroom. It provides the best learning environment, uses the best methods, and takes the lessons deep into our hearts.

Qualified for Service

Have you ever had the thought *God can't use me*? What was the disqualifier? Was it because of your lack of experience? Your education? Your personality? Your heritage? Your nationality? Not having the right look? Honestly, I've thought God couldn't use me on numerous occasions and for a variety of reasons. It seems I'm always disqualifying myself. Of course, I'm not alone in that. Moses, one of God's greatest leaders, didn't consider himself qualified for the position God was calling him to. When God called Moses into service, Moses recused himself by saying, "'O my lord, I am not eloquent, neither before nor since You have spoken to Your servant; but I am slow of speech and slow of tongue'" (Exodus 4:10). What was God's response? "'Who has made man's mouth?...Now therefore, go, and I will be with your mouth and teach you what you shall say'" (verses 11-12).

God told Moses in no uncertain words that He would be the qualifier. God, who made Moses's mouth, would qualify him for service. God would provide the eloquence, words, and authority needed to call, deliver, and lead the Israelites out of Egypt.

God is the qualifier. Just as God qualified Billy Sunday to become one of the foremost American evangelists, He qualified Moses, and He will qualify you! God qualifies the unqualified for His service! Paul took note of this awesome reality when he wrote to Timothy, a young pastor. In the first epistle to Timothy, Paul revealed the qualifying power of God's grace to him. God transformed Paul from "a blasphemer, a persecutor, and an insolent man" to "enabled" and put him into the ministry (1 Timothy 1:12-13). Concerning this qualifying work of God, he writes, "The grace of our Lord was exceedingly abundant, with faith and love which are in Christ Jesus" (verse 14).

If God could do that for Paul, who called himself chief of sinners, just think what He desires to do in your life! Paul continued, "For this reason I obtained mercy, that in me first Jesus Christ might show all longsuffering, as a pattern to those who are going to believe on Him for everlasting life" (verse 16). Paul wrote that he was cho-sen by God to give hope to any and all who came to Jesus by faith. In other words, Paul's rationale was this: If God can save me and qual-ify me for service, He can save and qualify anyone!

What have you allowed to disqualify you from God's service? Was it a discouraging word? I've met a myriad of women to whom or about whom some ugly statement was spoken. For years they identified themselves by that statement rather than by the grace of God. What a rip-off!

I have a friend who for years hesitated to become involved in ministry. She felt a tugging on her heart from God, but every time she started to step into ministry she remembered an ominous word spoken over her by a pastor when she was a young woman. He'd said, "You will never do anything great for God." Can you imagine someone saying that? Well, she believed it, and she limited her par-ticipation because of that word.

One day, quite by accident, she was propelled into ministry and used almost immediately in a tremendous way. This opportunity opened the door for more and more service. Soon she was leading a prayer meeting, teaching at retreats, and speaking at various venues. She confided to me that for a long time she let this negative word define the borders of her spiritual activity. As she was sharing with me, another woman overheard, and she, too, shared a negative word that had once kept her from active ministry.

Have you had a negative word spoken over you? Have you allowed that word to define the parameters of your qualification for God's service? God's grace is greater and speaks a greater word over you!

A woman at my church liked to critique every study I taught. A beautiful bouquet of flowers always accompanied her letters, but the critique was excoriating. She found fault with my clothes, my demeanor, my delivery, and of course, my message. Every missive began with *Dearest Cheryl*. In one of her communications, she told me I wasn't truly saved and I'd never be unless I went under her strict tutelage. Although I knew the woman wasn't mentally sound, her words still rocked me. I could take criticism about my clothes, my hair, my demeanor, and everything else, but I couldn't fathom being disqualified by God. If loving God, His Word, and the work of Jesus Christ wasn't enough, what was?

The day after I received one of her letters, my personal devotions had me in the first chapter of Colossians. As I read, all my misgivings gave way to joy. There in Colossians 1:12, Paul wrote about "giving thanks to the Father who has qualified us to be partakers of the inheritance of the saints in the light." That was my word from God. The Father through Christ had qualified me, and no one could take that from me. I'm not qualified by wearing the right clothes, by being eloquent, or by perfect behavior, but I am qualified by faith in the perfect work of Jesus Christ on my behalf.

The same is true for you. You're not qualified because you received the perfect education, went to the perfect schools, have the perfect friends, always behave perfectly, wear the perfect clothes, or always say the perfect thing. You're qualified because you believe in the perfect work of the only perfect Son of Man on your behalf. This is the grace that qualifies us by faith in God's perfect work for us.

Hebrews 10 explores the means by which Jesus has qualified us to God. He has done it by His own perfect blood. He died on our behalf, offering His own body as a sacrifice for our sins. Then He took that perfect blood into the Holy of Holies, the very throne room of God, and presented it as an atonement for our sins. Jesus's blood didn't just cover our sins; it forgave our sins. His gift was so perfect that it forgave, purified, and qualified us to God. This was evidenced by the tearing of the curtain that barred the way to the Holy of Holies. Jesus granted us access to the throne of grace! We did not and cannot qualify ourselves. Our confidence in our qualifications is not because of who we are or what we've done, but rests entirely on who Jesus is and what He has done!

Transforming Grace

Are you ready for a quiz? Let's see if you can guess the answer. What song is sung over ten million times a year all over the world and has been recorded over 11,000 times? It's "Amazing Grace," written by John Newton! This is undoubtedly the most well-known, well-sung, and well-loved hymn of all time. Its allure is the transforming and qualifying power of grace.

Perhaps you've read John Newton's testimony.[2] He was born in London in 1725. His mother, who taught him to read the Bible, died when he was only seven, and his strict seafaring father raised him. John began to accompany his father on voyages when he was 11, and at 19 he was press-ganged into service for the Royal Navy. John attempted to desert the navy, but he was caught and flogged. Then he managed to get himself transferred to a slave trade ship. For the next few years he became more and more immoral, impoverished, and degraded.

Then on a storm-tossed voyage from Brazil to Newfoundland, Newton was sure he would be swept overboard. He cried out to God for mercy, and God answered. Yet not even then did the hardened slave trader truly repent. He continued in the accursed trade for nine more years, incurring many near-death experiences—mutinous slave uprisings, fevers, storms—and many backslidings. Newton often retracted his faith, only to reclaim it when his life was threatened.

Finally, God's conviction began to overwhelm him, and he started to loathe his trade and everything associated with it. Although he quit his maritime occupation, he still felt accursed by his former trade. Then he met George Whitefield, the famous open-air preacher of England. Newton accompanied Whitefield as much as possible. When he wasn't with him, he was studying the Bible and fellowshipping in several small congregations, seeking to grow and be established in the faith. In 1764 Newton was ordained and made a curate in a small church in Olney, England. He remained in the parish until his invitation to be the rector of St. Mary Woolnoth in London in 1779.

During his time in Olney, John Newton wrote several hymns. He used them in many of his sermons to undergird the biblical assimilation of the principle he was teaching. He found hymns especially effective in teaching children the gospel, which was one of his greatest passions. One of the last hymns he wrote in Olney was "Amazing Grace." It was not only a testimony of his life, but also a doctrinal statement about the divine quality of grace.

> Amazing grace! How sweet the sound
> That saved a wretch like me!
> I once was lost, but now am found;
> Was blind, but now I see.
>
> 'Twas grace that taught my heart to fear
> And grace my fears relieved;
> How precious did that grace appear
> The hour I first believed.
>
> Through many dangers, toils, and snares,
> I have already come;
> 'Tis grace that brought be safe thus far,
> And grace will lead me home.

The Lord has promised good to me,
His word my hope secures;
He will my Shield and Portion be,
As long as life endures.

Yea, when this flesh and heart shall fail,
And mortal life shall cease,
I shall possess, within the veil,
A life of joy and peace.

The earth shall soon dissolve like snow,
The sun forbear to shine;
But God, who called me here below,
Will be forever mine.

When we've been there ten thousand years,
Bright shining as the sun,
We've no less days to sing God's praise
Than when we'd first begun.

John Newton did not have a perfect past. He wrote in his own epitaph,

John Newton, clerk, once an infidel and libertine, a
servant of slaves in Africa, was, by the rich mercy
of our Lord and Saviour Jesus Christ, preserved,
restored, pardoned, and appointed to preach the faith
he had long laboured to destroy.

Even after John Newton made his first commitment to Christ, he continued to fail miserably until that fateful day when God called him to account and to follow Him completely.

Perhaps you've had a series of backslidings or failings. You think you've gone beyond the grace of God. Think again. God's wonderful grace is higher than the mountains and deeper than the sea, and it reaches out to you and to me!

Now, I think I know what you might be thinking: *Billy Sunday, Paul the apostle, and even John Newton did those things before they met Jesus. But I've done some awful things since I met Jesus—things that should disqualify me.* So? God's grace has no limits to forgiveness, cleansing, transforming, and qualifying. Consider Peter, the apostle. After Jesus called him to be His apostle, Peter declined, saying, "Lord, depart from me. I'm a sinful man" (Luke 5:8, paraphrased). The Bible records those times when Peter got it wrong. He even tried to rebuke Jesus (Matthew 16:22). Imagine that! Jesus said to him, "'Get behind Me, Satan!'" (verse 23). Whoa! That's a pretty big mistake, wouldn't you say?

Then again, we read in Matthew 17, where, in a moment of absolute glory, Peter spoke out of turn. There he was in the presence of Moses and Elijah and beholding Jesus's glory (Matthew 17:1-5). Mark records that Peter said this "because he did not know what to say, for they were greatly afraid" (verse 6). Then in verse 7 God thundered from the cloud at Peter, "'This is My beloved Son. Hear Him!'"

Peter was among the disciples who tried to keep the children from coming to Jesus (Matthew 19:13-14). He was also among the consortium that criticized Mary when she anointed Jesus's feet (Matthew 26:6-13). He was the one who at first refused to let Jesus wash his feet (John 13:1-10). He also boasted that he was better than the other disciples and would never deny Jesus (Mark 14:29-31). He fell asleep in the garden of Gethsemane after Jesus asked him to watch and pray (Mark 14:37-41). At Jesus's arrest, Peter cut off the ear of the high priest's servant (John 18:10). He's also the disciple who denied that he knew Jesus not once, but three times (John 18:15-27).

Yet none of these failures, lapses, or outright sins disqualified Peter for service. Jesus knew Peter would fail; he even warned Peter of his coming failure: "'Simon, Simon! Indeed, Satan has asked for you, that he may sift you as wheat. But I have prayed for you, that your faith should not fail; and when you have returned to Me, strengthen your brethren'" (Luke 22:31-32).

Jesus knew Peter better than Peter knew himself. Jesus knew Peter would fail, but that failure would not keep him from the commission the Lord had for him. Afterward, when Peter had returned to Jesus, the commission to strengthen his brethren would be waiting for him to fulfill because of and by God's grace.

Peter should have known better. Peter should have done better. After all, he had walked in the presence of Jesus for three years and seen Him perform miracle after miracle. He'd even walked on water to Jesus (Matthew 14:29). Yet Peter failed miserably on more than one occasion.

Perhaps you also should have known better, should have done better. After all, you've been walking with the Lord a long time and been a recipient of God's goodness. Yet you failed miserably. The good news is that God's grace continues to forgive, cleanse, transform, and qualify you for the commission God has for you. You are not beyond the infinite grace of God!

One day there was a knock at my front door. I opened it to find a dear friend of mine in tears. After deciding to leave her husband, she had walked to my house. I couldn't believe it! I invited her to sit down on my couch, and I offered her a cup of tea, which she gladly accepted. She began to pour out the saga of the last few weeks of her life. Her marriage had been unfulfilling for a long time. Her husband was known to flirt with women at church, and at the same time he was never short of disparaging comments about her. His only exercise, by his own admission, was working his thumb on the TV remote control.

Because finances were tight, my friend had taken a job at a local store. There she met a wonderful Christian young man. He was everything a godly man should be, and a friendship developed between them. Soon she found herself enveloped by thoughts about him, and she began to feel attracted to him. Eventually she felt compelled to confess her attraction to him, and he was deeply displeased. He not only rebuked her, but threatened to tell her husband. My friend knew she had to confess everything to her husband. When she did, he flew into a rage. He called her all sorts of degrading names. His hostility was so great that my friend fled the house for her life and came to mine.

I told her I totally understood how she could be attracted to her coworker, especially given the condition of her marriage. She looked at me astonished. "No!" she declared. "I have always been a good, faithful, and loving wife. I don't know what came over me!"

I started to laugh. Perhaps it was the tension of the moment. Then I replied, "No. You've never been that good. God's grace was simply keeping you and holding you back. Your good character and behavior have been by the grace of God. God just let you go for a moment so you would know what your human nature is capable of and maybe to scare your husband into appreciating you more."

I don't know if my words were prophetic, but within hours her husband was calling our house and humbly asking to speak with his wife. He apologized profusely. It seemed that while she and I were talking and praying, God was dealing with him in no uncertain terms. He realized how awful he'd treated her, and they both moved to improve their marriage.

All this to say, you're never out of the reach of your sin nature.

It's always there, ready to take advantage of your weaknesses. You'll never reach perfection on earth. Like Peter, you'll blow it again and again. Yet just as it did for Peter, God's grace will be waiting to forgive, cleanse, transform, reinstate, and qualify you for His good work.

Yes, Jesus's grace is worth fighting for! It's worth battling against all the disqualifying voices. It's worth fighting against our own feelings of unworthiness and instead pressing into His amazing grace.

God's grace can qualify you for His service. His grace calls, forgives, cleanses, transforms, and qualifies us for His glorious plans.

....

Lord, thank You for the power of Your grace. Thank You that by Your grace You have forgiven and cleansed me from all my sin. Please help me to allow grace to continue to change and transform my life. Silence all the voices that condemn me and try to limit the power of grace in me. Thank You that You have qualified me by the perfect life and perfect sacrifice of Jesus so I can be used for Your great glory. In the name of the gracious Lord Jesus, amen.

For consideration:

1. List some of the reasons you've felt unqualified for God's service.

2. What evidence of the transforming grace of God have you seen in your own life?

3. Why do you think grace is a better teacher than the law?

4. In what areas of your life do you need to see the transforming grace of God?

5. Read 1 Timothy 1:12-17 and briefly recount Paul's testimony of grace. Write down any similarities you find between Paul's testimony and your own.

6. If you were to write a hymn about God's grace in your life, what would you title it?

Six

The Armory of Grace

*Let the word of Christ dwell in you richly in all wisdom, teaching
and admonishing one another in psalms and hymns and
spiritual songs, singing with grace in your hearts to the Lord.*

COLOSSIANS 3:16

Beginning in the 1700s and into the 1900s, over 22 armories for the volunteer militia were built in New York City. These structures were so well built that most of them, though no longer used for weapon storage, still stand today. At the time of their construction, the nation's leaders recognized the need for strong, fortified, and well-guarded buildings to store, maintain, and supply the local militia in case of an enemy attack.

Many people choose to build personal armories in their homes in the event of some catastrophic event. The owners have stocked them with weapons, food, water, clothing, and other necessities of life. These personal armories are carefully guarded, stockpiled, and maintained.

We all have an internal armory. We guard it. We stock it with supplies. We maintain it. What is this armory? Our heart, of course!

Our heart contains a surplus of memories, principles, defense mech-
anisms, and plans. The heart is where we store everything important to us. The heart is not only the physical supply of oxygen for
our whole body, but from a spiritual standpoint, it's the divine supply of everything we need for life and godliness.

What's the issue, then? The issue is what's being stored in your
heart! Some of the old armories in New York City have been turned
into housing. Others, though empty, are uninhabitable because of
the dangerous chemical nature of some of the weapons they once
contained.

Our hearts are the ultimate storage unit of our lives. Some hearts
contain an arsenal of lethal weaponry. These stored weapons are
continually poisoning the heart and making it uninhabitable. The
Bible issues clear warning about the arsenal of the heart. Proverbs
4:23 says, "Keep your heart with all diligence, for out of it spring the
issues of life." Is your heart filled with the supplies that would sustain you and strengthen you through a catastrophic event?

Heart Problems

I've got some bad news for you: Your heart, like mine, has a natural inclination away from God and goodness rather than toward
them. God put it this way through His prophet Jeremiah: "'The
heart is deceitful above all things, and desperately wicked; who
can know it?'" (Jeremiah 17:9). Jesus, in speaking of the heart,
said, "'From within, out of the heart of men, proceed evil thoughts,
adulteries, fornications, murders, thefts, covetousness, wickedness,
deceit, lewdness, and an evil eye, blasphemy, pride, foolishness. All
these evil things come from within and defile a man'" (Mark 7:21-
23). This definitely doesn't sound like a healthy armory, does it?

We all have a natural bent toward storing in our heart things not
healthy for us emotionally, mentally, or even physically. The storage

unit in the heart will govern our thoughts, and consequently our outlook on life and our responses to the events of life.

What, then, is the good news? Jesus wants to clear out the storehouses of our hearts. He wants to get rid of all the dangerous weapons, poisons, and expired items. He wants to cleanse our armories, completely ridding them of any residue from the toxins they once stored.

Return with me again to the good news of 1 John 1:9: "If we confess our sins, He is faithful and just to forgive us our sins and to cleanse us from all unrighteousness." Not only is God willing to forgive us the sins of our hearts, but He desires to wash them clean. God removes all the traces of unrighteousness from our hearts. His cleansing is thorough. Then He goes a step further and fills our hearts with His grace!

A New Armory

Before you knew Jesus, you needed to protect yourself from the world. Every time your feelings were hurt, every time your trust was violated, every time you were cast aside, your heart stored it. Then your heart began to develop weaponry against the aggressors of life. The problem was that the heart began to lose the ability to discern between who was an enemy and who was a friend. You used the weapons of your heart indiscriminately. The reserves of the heart weren't life-imparting or life-sustaining. They hurt others, and they damaged you as well.

Ever hear the term "a piece of my mind"? We all know that phrase means telling someone off, demeaning him or her, lashing out. I don't know about you, but never have I given away a "piece of my mind" when I didn't then want to retrieve those brain cells. The gratification was short-lived and gave way to immense shame, embarrassment, and oodles of condemnation.

That was your old armory. You needed those weapons for survival. Once you come to Jesus, however, He takes responsibility for your protection. One of my father's favorite hymns was "Day by Day." This hymn contains these wonderful stanzas:

> Every day the Lord Himself is near me,
> With a special mercy for each hour;
> All my cares He fain would bear and cheer me,
> He whose name is Counselor and Power.

> The protection of His child and treasure
> Is a charge that on Himself He laid;
> "As thy days, thy strength shall be in measure,"
> This the pledge to me He made.

Oh, how I love those lyrics! What a comfort they are to me. Jesus has undertaken the protection of our hearts. He laid this charge on Himself. We don't have to toughen our hearts or store defensive and offensive toxins anymore. Because Jesus is the Sovereign of our heart, He wants to fill our armories with new supplies. Second Corinthians 10 speaks about these new weapons: "Though we walk in the flesh, we do not war according to the flesh. For the weapons of our warfare are not carnal but mighty in God for pulling down strongholds, casting down arguments and every high thing that exalts itself against the knowledge of God, bringing every thought into captivity to the obedience of Christ" (2 Corinthians 10:3-5).

Emptying the Old Arsenal

I'll never forget my wedding day. Since the ceremony was in the evening, the day was filled with last-minute errands. My aunt E.C. volunteered to go hither and thither with me to finish the details and pick up my wedding dress, all tailored and pressed. We also volunteered to pick up hamburgers for everyone getting ready at my parents' house.

E.C. wanted to talk to me about my fiancé. In the car she said, "Now, honey, I want a straight answer. Why do you want to marry Brian Brodersen?" Of course, I was attracted to Brian, and I loved him. But E.C. was asking for more than that. She was probing for the reason I was linking my life forever with Brian's. I was ready with the answer. "E.C., when I'm with Brian, I can be the woman I've always wanted to be. I can be real, and I can be kind."

Before knowing Brian, I had built a wall around myself. I'd been hurt once too often, and I'd created a protective shield around my heart. I was often curt and cold to unwanted suitors. It wasn't that I thought less of them, but I knew they weren't right for me. Now that Brian was in my life, I could empty the arsenal of my heart from the defensive weaponry. I would now have the security of identity as Brian's wife.

In the same regard, a covenant with Jesus gives us the grace to be the person we long to be. Covenanted with Him, we no longer have to protect ourselves from the cruelties of life. He protects us. He empties our warehouse of weapons, cleanses it, and prepares it to be the house of His grace.

Filled with Grace

It happened during a specific crisis, when I learned some terrible news about one of my children. I tried to calm myself so I could deal rationally, calmly, and effectively with my child and the offense. I searched my body for a calm button but found I had only panic buttons. The more I tried to calm myself, the more my frustration increased. In that state, I had no way to deal productively with the situation. In utter despair I cried out to the Lord. "I have nothing in the inventory of my heart to deal with this situation. I'm empty."

God heard my prayer. Through the venue of His grace, He calmed my spirit.

It was a process. First, He began to show me what was causing me to panic. At the base of everything in my heart was fear. I was so afraid for my daughter. Second was my love for control. I wanted some physical means to fix her. I wanted a lecture, a locked door, a restriction, or some punishment that would change her mind and ways. I had tried all these before, though, and they were not only ineffective but counterproductive. Since my schemes had failed, I was in a panic. Fear gripped me and wouldn't let me rest.

God spoke to me and told me to surrender these things in my heart to Him. I did. I didn't just surrender my fear but all my failed methodology and my desire for control. God didn't leave an empty space. No. He filled me with His grace. His grace calmed me. His grace filled my heart and reminded me of everything He had done. His grace assured me He would work.

My attitude changed. The panic ceased. I was no longer desperately looking for some means to remedy the situation. Rather, I was filled with the grace I needed to endure, speak graciously, and act graciously. God not only changed the atmosphere of my heart; He changed the atmosphere of my home. This change of atmosphere even affected my daughter. I can honestly say grace gave her the opportunity to change as well.

God wants to fill your heart with His grace. He wants your heart to become an armory of grace. In Luke 6:45 Jesus said, "'Out of the abundance of the heart [a good man's] mouth speaks.'" If our hearts are filled with panic, anger, and frustration, our speech will reflect those attitudes, and those attitudes will color the atmosphere around us. If our hearts are filled with grace, however, we will draw upon grace and speak grace, and grace will permeate the atmosphere.

One of my favorite verses is Proverbs 11:16: "A gracious woman retains honor." Nothing is quite as humiliating as losing honor. We lose honor when the armories of our hearts are filled with anything other than God's grace.

To be able to draw from the reserves of grace is awesome. Grace is the divine supply of anything and everything you need for any given situation. Writing about grace, Paul said, "God is able to make all grace abound toward you, that you, always having all sufficiency in all things, may have an abundance for every good work" (2 Corinthians 9:8). Observe the totality of grace. Grace is the divine insurance policy that covers every inevitability. Nothing is omitted by grace. It's all grace. No element of grace is left out.

What do you need for your situation? Do you need love? Grace supplies it. Do you need wisdom? Grace will give it to you. Do you need peace? It's there in grace. Do you need faith? Grace will supply it. Do you need joy? You'll discover it in grace.

God's grace not only meets the need; it abounds toward us. Grace produces more grace. The New Living Translation translates John 1:16 like this: "From his abundance we have all received one gracious blessing after another." Peter opens his epistles with "Grace to you and peace be multiplied" (1 Peter 1:2) and "Grace and peace be multiplied to you" (2 Peter 1:2). Yes! Grace multiplies. Grace grows grace.

Grace always works. Grace never fails. You can never go to the armory of grace and find that it has run out of grace. Unlike an aged weapon, God's grace is never defective. His grace continually and effectively works for every situation.

Everything you endeavor to do, you do by grace and with grace. Everything that happens to you is infused with grace. Here is the supply house of "all sufficiency." As the song "Wonderful Grace of

Jesus" chorused, "all sufficient grace for me, for even me!" God's grace meets every need. It's the perfect solution, perfect weapon, and perfect supply for everything you need.

Grace doesn't barely meet the need or even simply cover the need. No! Grace goes beyond the need with an overage, with an "abundance of grace for every good work" (2 Corinthians 9:8). Grace surrounds, encases, and fills the atmosphere. When Jesus fed the multitudes, as recorded in Matthew 14 and 15, everyone who ate was filled. Every hungry appetite was satiated. Even more than that, however, 12 baskets held leftovers when He fed the 5000 with five loaves and two fish, and seven large baskets held leftovers when Jesus fed the 4000 with seven loaves and a few little fish (Matthew 14:13-21; 15:32-38). The grace of Jesus reaches the need and leaves leftovers of grace—more than enough grace for everyone to partake, be satisfied, and take some home!

Hubert Mitchell took note of this grace before he moved his family of five to Indonesia in 1934. They were going there to evangelize the Kubu tribe, a tremendous endeavor, especially in those days. The area they were moving to was unknown to foreigners and dangerous. Neither Hubert nor his wife, Helen, knew the language of the tribe. Being accompanied by their three children would only increase their vulnerability to sickness, injury, and distraction. Yet they had heard and felt the call of God, and they were going. The journey by boat would be long and complicated, with many hours of sailing. No easy return to the comforts of America would be possible. Once they settled in Indonesia, even their communication with the outside world would be stymied and delayed.

Before setting sail, Hubert visited a pastor. There on the wall of the minister's office was a framed poem by Annie Johnson Flint titled "He Giveth More Grace." Hubert was so touched by it that he went straight to a nearby piano, and music to the beautiful words flowed from his heart to his fingers. He kept a copy of the poem on a piece of paper tenderly folded in his pocket and carried it with him at all times, often pulling it out to reread the words until he knew them by heart.

Hubert and his family made it safely to South Sumatra, where they set up a fledging missionary post. God gave Hubert favor with the Kubu tribe, and he began to learn their language and communicate the gospel of grace to them.

In 1940, Helen gave birth to their fourth child in the home of a local Dutch family that had access to a doctor. Two days after little Jean Marie was born, Helen's head began to ache severely, and two days later she died. Hubert was heartbroken. Yet in this remote place with his newborn baby girl and three other little ones to comfort, Hubert felt the comfort of God's grace.[1] At Helen's funeral, held the same day she died, Hubert sang the words of the poem to the music he'd written. We know it today as the hymn "He Giveth More Grace."

> He giveth more grace when the burdens grow greater,
> He sendeth more strength when the labors increase:
> To added afflictions He addeth His mercy,
> To multiplied trials, His multiplied peace.
>
> His love has no limit His grace has no measure,
> His power no boundary known unto men;
> For out of His infinite riches in Jesus
> He giveth, and giveth, and giveth again.
>
> Fear not that thy need shall exceed His provision,
> Our God ever yearns His resources to share;
> Lean hard on the arm everlasting, availing;
> The Father both thee and thy load will upbear.

When we have exhausted our store of endurance,
When our strength has failed ere the day is half done,
When we reach the end of our hoarded resources
Our Father's full giving has only begun.

In the darkest hour of Hubert Mitchell's life, he found the secret of God's abundant grace. The sorrow of his circumstances did not change. However, amid the sorrow, the pain, and the agony, Hubert found God's grace. In a letter he wrote to his sister and brother-in-law, Hubert recounted his story and the grace he received that night. God's grace continued to sustain the grieving father. Grace comforted the little family and enveloped them.

Hubert was able to draw from his armory of grace. Grace was available. Grace was abundant. Grace was appropriate for the need!

You need an armory of grace for life. There's no better source to draw everything you need for life than the armory of grace. God desires to stockpile your heart with grace!

Filled with All Grace

Before you can defend yourself with your armory of grace, you need to fill it up! This will require an emptying of the other occupants stored in the warehouse of your heart. I already testified about how I had to empty the fear and fix-it weapons of my heart to make room for the grace.

Cleaning anything is always a battle, isn't it? My first reaction to cleaning is not positive. I clean because things need to be cleaned and I like the result, but I can't say I enjoy doing laundry, washing dishes, dusting, or vacuuming. I have friends who enjoy those endeavors, but unfortunately I don't share their emotional response to cleaning. Cleaning means not being able to do what I want to do because I have to do what I need to do. I would much rather take my dog for a walk, have a conversation with a neighbor, go out with a friend, or play with my grandkids.

Sometimes I have to battle my emotions when it comes to cleaning. For instance, I have a wonderful barbecue, but it needs a weekly cleaning. The process is a bit involved. First, I have to take out the grate and place it in my kitchen sink. The grate is oily and filled with blackened residue that tends to get all over my counter, sink, and blinds. For this job I need rubber gloves, lots of soap, elbow grease, and time. Then a tray inside my barbecue is covered in foil that's torn and filled with the debris of past meals. So that must be removed and replaced with fresh foil. Now, for you cleaners, this might sound like fun, but for me it's pure drudgery, and I put it off as long as possible. However, if I put it off too long, my barbecue becomes inoperable. (I once left it too long and a fire broke out and consumed my chicken like a burnt sacrifice!)

In the same way, cleaning out our hearts isn't enjoyable. We have to recognize and deal with the daily filth accumulated there. We have to reckon with what's in our heart and acknowledge it, but, also, we have to let God clean it out!

I'll never forget a battle to simply admit the sin in my heart. I wanted Brian to get my car serviced. I was sure it had been almost a year since the last time, and the icons were beginning to light up on my dashboard. Brian's schedule was beyond busy, though, and he said he didn't have time that week to take it in.

We argued, and this was a fight I desperately wanted to win. I wanted the situation taken care of right away! As we quarreled, I felt myself losing the battle. He was sure the car had been serviced less than a year ago. I countered, "No. I have the receipt to show it was over a year ago."

He looked right at me and said gently, "Cheryl, I know that's a lie. You don't have the receipt." He was right. I didn't have it, but

I was sure one existed. I excused myself from the room and quietly snuck downstairs to find the elusive receipt. I searched everywhere, but it wasn't with the car receipts in the glove compartment of the car, it wasn't in the side door of the car, it wasn't in the trunk, and it wasn't in the lock box in the house that held our important documents.

While I searched, I felt the pressing conviction of my lie. The Lord clearly spoke to me. *Cheryl, I know you lied. Brian knows you lied. You know you lied. So why won't you simply confess it?*

Let me tell you something—it was such a battle to confess to Brian what we both knew. Crazy, huh? Yet what a battle ensued in my heart against admitting my sin! I was loath to admit it because I wanted to feel I was above lying. Obviously, I wasn't. Ugh! I wanted to have my car serviced, which I felt was a good motivation. Finally, I wanted to win the argument. In resisting the cleansing God wanted to give, I was in fact working against the very thing I wanted.

I confessed it to God. Then I confessed it to Brian, who quickly forgave me. He had known where the receipt was the whole time. It was in his office drawer. The car had been serviced nine months ago.

On a side note, Brian drove my car when we went to pick up our dog from a veterinarian appointment. While we were inside the vet's, someone left a card for car service on our windshield. Brian considered that a divine sign and took the car in for repairs. (It's working great, but it needs new tires.)

This is all to say it's not easy to admit sin. We want to think we're above it. We don't want to acknowledge the weapons in our heart as sin. Lying is a sin, but all sin is against God and an enemy to grace.

It's hard to clean out the old storage room because it's drudgery getting rid of the old, the corroded, and the toxins that reside in our heart. Sometimes they must be searched out and dismantled bit by bit. Grime spreads, and the job grows bigger even as we're cleaning.

We often have confidence in these decrepit weapons. Lying, cheating, and other sins become our go-to when circumstances get difficult and we want a quick fix. We must get rid of the old weapons that have never effectively worked. Also, these old weapons have the capacity to misfire and blow up the whole armory.

We must ask God to come in and cleanse our hearts. David, the psalmist, prayed, "Create in me a clean heart, O God, and renew a right spirit within me" (Psalm 51:10 KJV). David made this request to God when he'd been caught in sin and hadn't confessed it until after the prophet Nathan called him out on it. David realized the need in his heart to be cleansed so that a right spirit could be renewed in him. Before we can have the right spirit of grace, the armory of our heart needs a good cleansing. Once the heart is cleansed, it can be restocked with grace! We must find the storehouse of grace and begin to fill our hearts with it.

First, we go to the throne of grace. This is the throne highlighted in Hebrews 4:16: "Let us therefore come boldly to the throne of grace, that we may obtain mercy and find grace to help in time of need." This is the same throne the enemies of grace want to cut you off from by the various tactics we talked about in a previous chapter.

Prayer is the supply line of grace, taking us into the very throne room and making our need known. As we pray, God gives us the ample supply of grace to take back to our hearts. But prayer is a battle, isn't it? We don't always feel like praying. Often we think of a million things we need to do. Prayer takes time. Prayer is confession. Prayer is a conversation with God. This means we need a time in prayer to listen intently for God to speak to us after we have spoken to Him. We battle to pray so we can be filled with God's grace.

Another supply of grace comes from God's Word. The Bible is filled with grace. Luke 4:22 states that the citizens of Nazareth marveled at the "gracious words" Jesus spoke. God's Word imparts grace to our hearts. Colossians 3:16 instructs us on how to fill our hearts with God's gracious Word: "Let the word of Christ dwell in you richly in all wisdom, teaching and admonishing one another in psalms and hymns and spiritual songs, singing with grace in your hearts to the Lord." Here is the means by which to fill our hearts with the Word of God's grace:

First, we allow God's Word in. We don't just hear it; we ingest it. James 1:21 further instructs us to "receive with meekness the implanted word, which is able to save your souls." To allow it in, we must receive it with meekness. Meekness is the attitude of receptivity, the placement of God's Word in our hearts. We read it daily and seek to fill our minds and hearts with it.

Second, we use God's Word. We go to the storehouse of grace to get the supplies of grace found in God's Word to exercise the wisdom, to teach, and to warn others. We not only stock and restock our hearts with God's Word, but we go to this armory and make use of the supplies in it. We learn by using the Word we've been given. The more I use my computer, the more I understand it, and the more I want to use it. The same is true of God's Word. The more we use the Word He's given to us, the more we'll know His Word, and the more we'll want to use His Word.

Third, we learn the Word through psalms, hymns, and spiritual songs. Isn't it wonderful the way a song will fill your heart? Have you ever been strengthened by a song? I have on numerous occasions!

Coming into church one evening, I was overly burdened for one of my children. She had been making a series of poor choices that were jeopardizing her future, and she had left our home in a blaze of anger. I really didn't want to be in church that night, but I had nowhere else to go. Staying at home was not an option; it would only isolate me. So there I was at church. The worship began, and begrudgingly I sang along with the congregation, feeling no ability to feign or drum up an emotional response to the music. Then came the chorus to the second song, "Our God saves! Our God saves!" Suddenly my heart was filled with hope as I remembered the saving grace of God. This song became my anthem to the very day of my daughter's salvation!

I can recall many times when God used a song to fill the armory of my heart with His grace. Notice that in Colossians 3:16 Paul mentions three distinct types of songs. The first is psalms. Psalms are prayers, and every psalm is a prayer. Often in the psalms of the Bible, the author is processing his thoughts, amending his perspective, and then filling his heart with God's grace. Many of the psalms begin with a dilemma but end with a surge of glory as the author pours out his heart to God.

Other psalms are called declarative psalms. These psalms recount the work of God in the history of people's lives. As we rehearse the faithful work of God through the lives of the psalmists, our own armories are filled with grace!

Last are the imprecatory psalms. I particularly like these psalms. They're battle psalms. They call God's wrath down upon the Enemy while proclaiming the surety of God's victory.

So psalms fill the armory of our hearts with the grace of God. They allow us to pour out in song our problems, remind ourselves of His past faithfulness, and proclaim the certainty of His victory in our lives.

Paul then mentions a third type of song—the spiritual song. These are the choruses of the church. They tend to be more personal. They are often instructional. They inspire us with biblical themes such as love, faith, and joy. They usually have fewer lyrics and repeat phrases we need to store in the armory of our hearts.

A fourth type of song is hymns. I grew up singing hymns. It was not unusual to come home from school and find my mom at her piano playing one hymn after another. She would often invite me to sing while she accompanied me. Some of the greatest doctrinal statements found in Scripture are in those hymns, as well as in the hymns of the early church. During that time, parchment was expensive, most of society was illiterate, and not everyone could own a copy of the Scriptures. The early church fathers put the essential doctrines of the Bible into hymns so everyone could have the Word of God in their hearts.

Fellowship

Fellowship is an essential way to fill the storehouses of our hearts. When we meet with others, we get an opportunity to both extend and receive God's grace. We share testimonies, encourage one another with Scriptures, and sing songs.

Often God has used another person to remind me of His grace toward me. I can so easily slip into self-condemnation. At these times I need a brother or sister in the Lord to lift me out of it with a word of grace. Note that in Colossians 3:16, Paul said we are to teach and admonish one another.

Some people isolate themselves from the rest of God's children. The more you isolate yourself from fellowship, however, the more exclusive and graceless you'll become. Fellowship allows us to exercise grace, pull from the resources of grace in our hearts, and receive stockpiles of grace from Christians to restock our supplies. Proverbs 18:1 reads, "A man who isolates himself seeks his own desire; he rages against all wise judgment." Our armory of grace needs to also collect supplies of grace from others. They often give us the grace missing from our own storehouses.

Paul defines fellowship in Romans 1:11-12 when he writes, "I long to see you, that I may impart to you some spiritual gift, so that you may be established—that is, that I may be encouraged together with you by the mutual faith both of you and me." Fellowship is when we gather with other believers for the purpose of imparting a spiritual gift. It builds up our armories when together we're encouraged in our mutual faith in Christ Jesus.

Sometimes fellowship itself can be a battle, can't it? Sometimes it can seem as though everything in life is conspiring together to keep you from going to church. You can't find the clothes you hoped to wear, your kids get into a fight, the car won't start, you disagree with your husband, you find out someone you don't like is going to be there, you feel too tired to go, or some other distraction impedes your way. It's a battle, because Satan doesn't want you to receive the necessary supply of grace waiting for you as you fellowship with the saints. One of his chief tools for draining the armory of grace is to keep you from meeting with other believers.

The Benefits of an Armory Full of Grace

God wants to fill the armory of your heart with grace so you'll always have what you need for every situation. Rather than drawing from old, defunct, and dangerous weapons, when you go to the grace supply you'll find strength, comfort, joy, love, hope, and everything else necessary to help you in your time of need.

Annie Johnson Flint, the woman who wrote the poem "He Giveth More Grace," was herself a grace story. She was born in Vineland, New Jersey, to Eldon and Jean Johnson in 1866. Three years later her mother died while giving birth to her second daughter. At the same time, Annie's father was struck down with an incurable disease and had to give up custody of his little girls. Annie and her sister were adopted and taken into the Flint home. There they grew and matured in the atmosphere of God's grace, love, and Word. After Annie graduated from high school, she trained to become a schoolteacher. While she was still a teacher, her adoptive parents both died.

During her third year of teaching, she began to suffer from crippling pain. She was diagnosed with early onset arthritis and forced to resign her career, and became an invalid at a young age. Every day required the provision of God's grace to accomplish even the simplest of tasks. Yet drawing from the armory of God's grace, she wrote poems and encouraging letters and published inspirational booklets. Her life of grace ministered grace to many others, and her poems were her personal testimony of drawing from the riches of God's grace. Many others are still ministered to by the supplies that came from the armory of her grace-filled heart.

I'm sure Annie Johnson Flint had a constant battle to keep the armory of her heart free of the toxins of resentment, bitterness, and frustration. Yet her battle was rewarded with reserves of grace that upheld her and ministered to others.[2]

Do you desire an armory of grace in your heart? When frustration, hard circumstances, and difficulties come knocking at your door, don't you long to meet them with the resources of God's grace?

It will take a battle. It will mean taking inventory of all that resides in your present armory. It will mean allowing God to clean it out. Then it will take a cooperative effort with Him to refill your heart with His grace through prayer, His Word, and fellowship with other believers.

....

Dear Lord, I pray that You will work in me—as it says in Philippians 2:13—to will and to do of Your good pleasure. Grant me a desire to have grace in my heart. I choose to open my heart wide to You and allow You to come in and remove and clean the toxins present there. Lead me to the supplies of the riches of Your grace. Open my arms wide to receive armloads of grace through prayer, Your Word, and fellowship. Please fill and make my heart an armory of Your grace! In the name of Jesus, amen.

For consideration:

1. How is your heart like an armory?
2. How would you describe some of the items in your armory?
3. What is your usual reaction when you're riled?
4. What do you find most compelling about grace?
5. Can you share a time when God has used the following to minister His grace to you?

   - Prayer
   - Scripture
   - Song
   - Another Christian

6. What steps do you need to take to fill the armory of your heart with grace?

Seven

The Champion of Grace

Of His fullness we have all received, and grace for grace. For the law was given through Moses, but grace and truth came through Jesus Christ.

JOHN 1:16-17

In the 1980s a certain song soared to the number-two spot of popular songs in Great Britain. In America, the same song made it to the top forties and was recorded at least three times by three different artists. It's been heard on 11 different television shows, used in six different movies, and is the background music for two video games. The song? "Holding Out for a Hero."

Jim Steinem and Dean Pritchard wrote the song. Although they're men, it's about a woman's dream or request for the companionship of someone who's beyond anyone she's seen, met, or knows. Captured in the lyrics of this song is the deep desire of every woman for a champion.

If we're honest with ourselves, we'll admit we've all longed for a hero. We want someone who's wonderful. He must be divine and not afflicted with the failures of men. We want him to be faithful, loving, heroic, kind, and gentle, and yet courageous and strong!

In our heart of hearts, however, we believe we're not worthy of such a hero. A hero deserves perfection—and we're far from perfect.

Yet there's hope. We have such a hero in Jesus Christ! Isaiah 9:6 describes our hero as "Wonderful, Counselor, Mighty God, Everlasting Father, Prince of Peace." Here is the hero we need! Here is the hero we long for! Here is the hero we have!

He is wonderful. He is divine. He takes our breath away. Nothing is like the quality of wonderful. It's beyond good, it's beyond what we hoped for, and so our Jesus is wonderful!

He is a counselor. He listens! Who hasn't longed for a man who will listen? There's something captivating about someone who will listen to you, who will listen to the same story over and over and never say "You already told me—a billion times!"

He is Mighty God. He has absolute strength and power. He is divine. He is absolutely good!

He is the Everlasting Father. He is eternal. He is constant. There is never a time when He isn't present and available. He's always there for us. He has all the attributes of a good father. He is faithful. He provides. He is kind. He is gentle. He is generous. He is giving.

He is the Prince of Peace. He is royalty. He is noble. He brings calm to every situation. He drives away fear and leaves serenity in its wake.

This is the hero we need. This is the hero we have in Jesus. He is our champion!

The Greek word for champion is *archegos*. It was used in Greek mythology to speak of the flawed hero, Hercules. The same word is used in the New Testament four times in reference to Jesus (Acts 3:15; 5:31; Hebrews 2:10; 12:2), and is translated "prince," "captain," and "author."

Though Jesus was God's Son and absolutely qualified to lead the battle of grace, He went through the training of grace. Jesus was made "perfect" or complete through suffering. He didn't receive His rank simply because He was God's Son. There was no nepotism here. Jesus is the champion because of all He endured. He lived an absolute obedient and righteous life. Through His righteous life of truth, He manifested the grace of God toward us.

In Philippians 2 Paul states that, though Jesus was in the "form of God," He "made Himself of no reputation, taking the form of a bondservant, and coming in the likeness of men...He humbled Himself and became obedient to the point of death, even the death of the cross" (verses 6-8). It was this act of absolute obedience that qualified Jesus to receive the order of Champion. Paul added, "God also has highly exalted Him and given Him the name which is above every name, that at the name of Jesus every knee should bow, of those in heaven, and of those on earth, and of those under the earth, and that every tongue should confess that Jesus Christ is Lord, to the glory of God the Father" (verses 9-11). Jesus is both our Champion and Lord!

In this chapter we'll be looking at Jesus's school of grace. Through His ministry on earth, He continually exercised grace so that He would fully qualify as the Champion of our salvation. As we peruse Jesus's different interactions, we'll observe the constancy of His grace.

Jesus and His Disciples

One of the most notable aspects of Jesus's grace is seen in whom He chose as the Twelve, His closest disciples. In His grace, He didn't choose perfect men—far from it. He chose from the ordinary class of men. Mark writes that Jesus chose these men so He could be with them, send them out as His representatives, and empower them to heal and cast out demons (Mark 3:13-15).

Consider these three crucial factors in the choosing of these men:

1. Jesus was going to spend time with them. Now, think of the people you would choose to accompany you every day for three years. I bet that narrows the spectrum quite a bit for you! Three years is a long time to be with the same group of people day after day after day. No doubt you would choose people who would bring the greatest benefit to you.

2. Jesus wanted to send these men out to represent Him. So wouldn't you think He'd choose men with dynamic personalities, good looks, and nobility?

3. These were the men in whom Jesus would invest His power and authority. They should be men who could handle power, right?

A closer examination of Jesus's choices reveals these 12 were not the type of men most people would choose to spend time with, have represent them, and invest their power and authority in.

Peter was a working-class fisherman. He had a salty mouth (Matthew 26:74). He rebuked Jesus (Matthew 16:22). He spoke out of turn (John 13:8). He was disrespectful at times (Mark 8:32). He was insensitive at spiritual moments (Luke 9:33). He competed with the other disciples (Matthew 26:33). He even denied that he ever knew Jesus (Matthew 26:69-74).

Andrew was Peter's brother, coming from the same working class Peter did. Not much is written about him in the Gospels, except that he took Peter, the lad with the two fish and five loaves, and the Greeks to Jesus (John 1:41; 6:8-9; 12:21-22).

Jesus nicknamed brothers James and John "Sons of Thunder" (Mark 3:17). These young men were known for their bad temperament. At one point they wanted to call down fire from heaven and destroy a Samaritan village (Luke 9:54-55). In my opinion, they certainly didn't seem like the safest men in which to invest divine power and authority. These brothers were also ambitious. Much to the dismay of the other disciples, they asked Jesus if they could have the prime positions at His right hand when He came into His kingdom (Mark 10:35-45). They went so far as to conspire with their mother, having her intercede with Jesus on their behalf for prized positions (Matthew 20:20-21).

Then there was Philip. After three years with Jesus, he still didn't understand the relationship of Jesus to the Father. Obviously, he wasn't listening or watching! Jesus said to him, "'Have I been with you so long, and yet you have not known Me, Philip? He who has seen Me has seen the Father; so how can you say, "Show us the Father?"'" (John 14:8-9). How frustrating to invest so much time, energy, and power into someone who doesn't know you even after three years!

Bartholomew is believed to be another name for Nathanael. Remember him? When Philip told Nathanael about Jesus, his response was, "'Can anything good come out of Nazareth?'" (John 1:46). Jesus identified him as a man "'in whom is no deceit'" (verse 47). That's a nice way to say Nathanael was a man who always said what he was thinking.

Matthew (or Levi) was a tax collector (Luke 5:27). No profession was more hated or despised in Israel. The tax collectors were known for their deceit, treachery, and lying. Matthew's closest friends were other tax collectors and great sinners (Matthew 9:9-10).

The disciple Thomas has been dubbed "Doubting Thomas" by the church for ages. The reason is obvious: Thomas was slow to catch on. When Jesus announced He was going to "wake" Lazarus, meaning He was going to raise him from the dead, Thomas interjected, "'Lord, if he sleeps he will get well'" (John 11:12). When

Jesus talked about His departure at the Last Supper, Thomas said to Him, "'Lord, we do not know where You are going, and how can we know the way?'" (John 14:5). Thomas also doubted the reality of Jesus's bodily resurrection. No matter whose report he'd heard, he still declared, "'Unless I see in His hands the print of the nails, and put my finger into the print of the nails, and put my hand into His side, I will not believe'" (John 20:25).

Thaddaeus (also called Judas, but who was not Judas Iscariot) was another choice Jesus made. This is the disciple who at the Last Supper discourse asked, "'Lord, how is it that You will manifest Yourself to us, and not to the world?'" (John 14:22). Here was a disciple who, after observing Jesus, spending time with Jesus, and listening to Jesus, still didn't understand Jesus's plan. How frustrating is that? He was like one of those individuals you read instructions to over and over, and then they look up at you and say, "What am I supposed to do, again?" or "I don't remember you telling me anything about this."

Another disciple Jesus chose was Simon. He was called the Zealot (Luke 6:15). Zealots in those days were obsessed patriots. They had one cause—to see Israel rid of her oppressors. Zealots believed in using whatever means necessary to achieve their objective, and they were known for their violent nature.

Not much is known about James, the Son of Alphaeus, except that he was one of the disciples and therefore shared in all their experiences and foibles.

Finally, we come to the notorious Judas Iscariot. From the beginning Jesus knew Judas would betray Him (John 13:11), yet He chose him to be one of the Twelve. He invested His word, time, power, and authority into him. Jesus even entrusted Judas with the money box (John 12:6). That's incredible grace!

All the men Jesus chose were imperfect. They competed with each other about who was the greatest (Mark 9:34); they criticized a woman's worship of Jesus (Matthew 26:6-9); and even after all the time they spent with Jesus, they lacked the faith to cast out a demon (Mark 9:17-19). They all forsook Jesus at His arrest in Gethsemane (Mark 14:50). Yet Jesus loved His flawed and decidedly human disciples to the uttermost (John 13:1).

Jesus didn't choose His disciples based on their social status, education, wealth, expertise, bravery, character, or discipline. He chose them simply so He could be with them, use them as His ambassadors, and invest in them. Jesus chose the disciples based on what He could and would do in them, not on who they were or what they had done.

The Champion of our salvation chooses based on His grace. Paul, in speaking of Jesus's choices, stated this:

> You see your calling, brethren, that not many wise
> according to the flesh, not many mighty, not many
> noble, are called. But God has chosen the foolish
> things of the world to put to shame the wise, and
> God has chosen the weak things of the world to put
> to shame the things which are mighty; and the base
> things of the world and the things which are despised
> God has chosen, and the things which are not, to
> bring to nothing the things that are, that no flesh
> should glory in His presence (1 Corinthians 1:26-29).

Again in 2 Timothy 1:9, Paul writes about the Lord as the One "who has saved us and called us with a holy calling, not according to our works, but according to His own purpose and grace which was given to us in Christ Jesus before time began." Jesus called the disciples for the purpose of what He could do for them rather than what they could do for Him. Jesus even chose Judas and gave him the same insights, opportunities, and love He gave the other disciples.

Today the Champion of our salvation chooses men and women He wants to dwell with. He chooses these individuals to bless them with His likeness and to invest His power and authority in them. That's grace!

Jesus and Sinners

The grace of the Champion of our salvation can be seen in His gracious attitude toward sinners. Jesus sought out and forgave sinners. After calling Matthew, the tax collector, to be His disciple, Jesus went to his house, sat down, and ate with known tax collectors and sinners. He proclaimed it wasn't the healthy who needed a physician, but the sick.

On another occasion Jesus sought out the worst tax collector in Jericho—Zacchaeus. This hated—and short—man wanted to catch a glimpse of Jesus despite the crowd around Him, so he climbed up in a sycamore tree. Imagine his surprise when the Messiah walked directly up to the tree he was perched in and called him by name! "'Zacchaeus, make haste and come down, for today I must stay at your house'" (Luke 19:5). After spending time in the house of Zacchaeus, Jesus announced, "'Today salvation has come to this house, because he also is a son of Abraham; for the Son of Man has come to seek and to save that which was lost'" (verses 9-10).

Mary Magdalene, who had once been possessed by seven demons (Luke 8:2), was a close follower of Jesus. She followed Him everywhere He went during His earthly ministry.

Once when Jesus was teaching in the court of the temple, He was interrupted by the Pharisees. They were a group of men who sought to scrupulously keep the law, and they had added commands to the Law of Moses that went beyond the righteousness of the law. They considered themselves superior to other men, and they thought they had merited the good favor of God by their works and self-efforts. They were also quick to condemn others.

On this day, they had in their clutches a woman who'd been caught "in the act of adultery" (John 8:3 NLT). They demanded that Jesus pronounce sentence on her, claiming, "'Now, Moses, in the law, commanded us that such should be stoned. But what do You say?'" (verse 5). Jesus acted as though He didn't hear these men's accusations. Silently, He stooped to the ground and began to write in the dirt with His finger. Then He stood up and announced, "'He who is without sin among you, let him throw a stone at her first.'" Stooping again, He continued to write on the ground. What He wrote isn't recorded; however, it's interesting to note that both the Ten Commandments in Exodus 20 and the words of judgment given to Belshazzar were written with the finger of God (Exodus 31:18; Daniel 5:5). Jesus alone had the right to condemn this woman, yet He chose to forgive her, even convicting and challenging her prosecutors in the process (John 8:1-11).

In the time of Jesus's ministry, any woman who had a menstrual issue was considered unclean. She wasn't even allowed to be in public when she was menstruating. Yet a woman who had suffered through 12 years of constant bleeding made her way through a maddening throng of people, reached out her hand, and touched the hem of Jesus's garment. The moment she made contact she was healed from her malady. Jesus immediately stopped and asked, "'Who touched Me?'" (Luke 8:45). The woman knew that, according to the law, she would be condemned for her infraction. Trembling, she fell before Jesus and confessed everything. No doubt she expected a public berating, but that wasn't what she received. Jesus looked at her and announced, "'Daughter, be of good cheer; your faith has made you well. Go in peace'" (verse 48).

Look at this display of grace! Jesus doesn't rebuke this woman. He doesn't censure her for touching Him in her unclean state. He doesn't retract her healing. Rather than condemning her, Jesus reestablishes her dignity as a daughter of Abraham, restores her joy, commends her faith, and sends her away in peace.

Throughout the Gospels, the grace of Jesus is on display. The Champion of our salvation forgives the undeserving, heals the helpless, cleanses the unclean, and delivers the captives by His grace. He allows the multitude to press in on Him. He continues to teach, minister, call out to, and provide for those who come with untoward motives and those who come in sincerity. He is gracious to all.

Jesus's Words of Grace

Oh, what gracious words our Lord spoke. When He went to the synagogue in Nazareth, those in attendance "marveled at the gracious words which proceeded out of His mouth" (Luke 4:22). In Luke 4:18-19, Jesus read from a portion in Isaiah 61:1-2 commonly identified with the Messiah. He said, "'The Spirit of the LORD is upon Me, because He has anointed Me to preach the gospel to the poor; He has sent Me to heal the brokenhearted, to proclaim liberty to the captives and recovery of sight to the blind, to set at liberty those who are oppressed; to proclaim the acceptable year of the LORD.'"

Jesus came with the good news (the gospel). He presented Himself as the One who would enrich the poor, heal the brokenhearted, and bring deliverance to the captives, sight to the blind, and freedom to the oppressed. He offered His services to the people of Nazareth. Jesus was saying, "I am here, and this is what I will do for you." It was a gracious offer, and the people marveled; they weren't used to hearing such a gracious offer. The religious elite in Jerusalem made demands of their time, activity, and money. Rome was constantly oppressing them with new laws and taxes. Jesus wasn't asking anything of them; rather, He was offering them hope, healing, and health.

Yet though they marveled at His words, they refused to receive Him as their Messiah. They even sought to push Him off the brow of a hill, but Jesus passed through their midst unharmed (Luke 4:16-30).

Jesus offered the multitudes rest and peace: "'Come to Me, all you who labor and are heavy laden, and I will give you rest. Take My yoke upon you and learn from Me, for I am gentle and lowly in heart, and you will find rest for your souls. For My yoke is easy and My burden is light'" (Matthew 11:28-30).

Jesus offered the people abundant life. "'The thief does not come except to steal, and to kill, and to destroy. I have come that they may have life, and that they may have it more abundantly'" (John 10:10).

Though the word of Jesus is powerful enough to calm seas, cast out legions of demons, and harness the powers of creation, He spoke words of grace to men. The Champion of our salvation—as the Son of God, the only truly righteous One—could have demanded allegiance, but instead He gave an invitation of grace.

Jesus and His Enemies

Think about how easily Jesus could have destroyed His enemies—those who hated Him, constantly scrutinized Him, criticized Him, condemned Him, and conspired against Him. Yet Jesus was patient with them. He never hid from them. He never spoke in secret. He reasoned with them and gave them every opportunity to repent. He countered their accusations with truth and wisdom. When they tried to ensnare Him, He challenged them from the Scriptures and warned them against their hardness of heart (Luke 20).

How many champions act as graciously as Jesus did? Those who rejected Jesus hated Him, twisted His words, sought to entrap Him, publicly slandered Him, and viciously attacked Him. Isaiah 26:10 states, "Let grace be shown to the wicked, yet he will not learn righteousness." It's one thing to show grace to someone you hope will repent, but it's nearly impossible to manifest grace to someone who's hardened against repentance. Yet Jesus showed unwavering grace to even those who would never repent.

Jesus in His Suffering

Jesus's grace was clearly seen when He refused to unleash His power against His tormentors. John records the power of Jesus's word in the garden of Gethsemane. When the soldiers and high priests came to arrest Him, He stepped forward and said, "'I am He'" (John 18:5). At these words the whole company that came to arrest Him fell to the ground. Jesus waited for these men to regain their footing. He allowed them to bind Him and lead Him to Annas's house. He endured the false testimony, the false accusations, the spitting, and the blows from their fists. He said nothing until He was adjured by the high priest to speak.

He was led to Pilate, the Roman governor. He remained silent before him while His accusers lied and demanded His crucifixion. Jesus remained calm. He was in absolute control as His opponents foamed at the mouth, screamed, and reviled Him. Pilate was astonished at His serenity. "'Do You not know that I have power to crucify You, and power to release You?'" he asked (John 19:10). Jesus was unlike any other defendant Pilate had seen. Jesus didn't argue with His enemies. He didn't defend Himself. He didn't beg for His life. He didn't curse His prosecutors.

Jesus had not lost any of His power or authority. At any point legions of angels would have come to His rescue. The Champion Himself could have called down fire and devoured His enemies. Jesus, simply with His word, could have thrown them to the ground. Yet Jesus restrained His strength.

He allowed Pilate's soldiers to flog Him. He was silent before Herod. He offered no resistance to the men who arrayed Him in a purple robe and mocked Him. He accepted the heavy wooden cross they laid on His frayed back. He carried it publicly before the masses in Jerusalem.

He was nailed to a cross, and there our Champion fought the foes of grace. Scripture tells us, "He has made [you] alive together with Him, having forgiven you all your trespasses, having wiped out the handwriting of requirements that was against us, which was contrary to us. And He has taken it out of the way, having nailed it to the cross. Having disarmed principalities and powers, He made a public spectacle of them, triumphing over them in it" (Colossians 2:13-15).

The Champion of our salvation bore our griefs. He carried our sorrows. He was wounded for our transgressions and bruised for our iniquities. The price for our peace was laid upon Him. The Lord laid on Jesus the iniquity of us all (Isaiah 53). This sacrifice of Jesus made grace available to all men! He died for our sins so we could receive the gift of God's grace.

In Romans 5 Paul emphasized what Jesus's suffering accomplished for us:

> Much more then, having now been justified by
> His blood, we shall be saved from wrath through
> Him. For if when we were enemies we were recon-
> ciled to God through the death of His Son, much

more, having been reconciled, we shall be saved by
His life…much more the grace of God and the gift
by the grace of the one Man, Jesus Christ, abounded
to many. And the gift is not like that which came
through the one who sinned. For if by the one man's
offense death reigned through the one, much more
those who receive abundance of grace and of the gift
of righteousness will reign in life through the One,
Jesus Christ (Romans 5:9-10,15-17).

The Champion of our salvation was resolute in His suffering.
He refused to free Himself so He could bring grace to all those who
believe in His name.

Resurrection

Our Champion, having defeated death, returned to His disciples and showed Himself alive by "many infallible proofs" (Acts 1:3).
He met two of them on the road to Emmaus. He walked with them
while they were downcast and rehearsing together all the strange
events that had transpired in Jerusalem that day. Without identifying Himself, Jesus joined their conversation. Graciously, He
took them through the Scriptures from Genesis to Malachi and
"expounded to them in all the Scriptures the things concerning Himself" (Luke 24:27). He accompanied them to dinner, and then He
vanished from their midst after He took the bread, blessed it, and
broke it.

He appeared to His disciples as they gathered in a locked room
and discussed the empty tomb. "Now as they said these things, Jesus
Himself stood in the midst of them, and said to them, 'Peace to you.'
But they were terrified and frightened, and supposed they had seen
a spirit" (Luke 24:36-37).

You can imagine their consternation. On the one hand they must have been overjoyed by the Lord's presence. But in the next moment they must have been terrified. Their Champion was greater than they had ever realized. They must have also felt the condemnation of their unbelief, their fear, and their failure.

Look at the grace of Jesus! He has no words of condemnation for His hapless disciples. Rather, He inspires them to faith. He opens their understanding. He blesses them (Luke 24).

He met them again on the shore of the Sea of Tiberias, or the Galilee. Peter and the other disciples must have grown restless waiting for Jesus, because Peter announced he was going fishing. The other disciples joined him, but it was another fruitless night on the Galilee. As morning dawned, their nets were empty. From the shadows of the shore a voice called, "'Children, have you any food?'" (John 21:5). Their hollow "No" echoed across the rippling waves.

Again, the voice from the shore spoke. "'Cast the net on the right side of the boat, and you will find some'" (verse 6). The disciples complied in one last attempt to catch breakfast. Suddenly the little boat dangerously listed, and the disciples almost lost their balance. The net was so full of fish that the boat was at a perilous tilt. John looked at Peter and said, "'It is the Lord!'" (verse 7). Peter, not one to wait on ceremony, dove into the water and swam to shore.

Jesus was waiting on the beach. He had a fire going and breakfast waiting. The other disciples steered the boat to shore and hauled the nets onto land. Then they came to warm themselves at the fire.

Again, there is no word of condemnation, but only the reinstatement to ministry. Jesus asked Peter three times, "'Do you love Me?'" Each time Jesus asked Peter to demonstrate that love by feeding and nurturing His sheep (John 21:15-17).

This is the grace our Champion lived out! Paul writes, "You know the grace of our Lord Jesus Christ, that though He was rich, yet for your sakes He became poor, that you through His poverty might become rich" (2 Corinthians 8:9).

Beware WWJD

If we make Jesus simply our example, we've done a disservice to grace. To try to follow the example of Jesus will leave us crushed. He alone is the Champion. We don't study Jesus as a champion to emulate. No way! He is the Champion to receive into our hearts. His grace must be our power supply.

Years ago my son, who was five, was given one of those WWJD bracelets. You know, the rubber bracelets with the initials that stood for What Would Jesus Do? The bracelet was to remind the person wearing it to weigh every action and reaction against the life and words of Jesus. My son took on an attitude of superiority when he donned that rubber bangle. Soon he was sitting in judgment of his sisters, his brother, his friends, his father, and yes, his mother too! It was not unusual to see him slowly shaking his head at one of us and holding up his arm to reveal the WWJD band. We felt the condemnation for our failure. For a full week we all tried to live outwardly like Jesus. We suppressed our true emotions. We kept our voices lowered when addressing one another. We smiled when we were displeased. We tried to ignore the mounting tension. All the while my little son acted superior to us all.

Mounting frustration finally broke at dinner when my oldest son couldn't hold it in any longer. He had tried to be perfect and failed miserably. Now he let his emotions go and freely expressed his pent-up anger. That was all it took to set the girls free too. They joined in against the little guy with the bracelet. I had no idea how much everyone had been suppressing.

My youngest son looked appalled at all of us. Before he could raise his arm in the air, though, his siblings began to list all his infractions that week. Now, he thought, the whole family was condemned. He tried to fight back as best a five-year-old could. He wasn't going down with them. He had the magic bracelet, and they didn't. But the bracelet wasn't making him righteous. It had created a hypocritical spirit in my boy. He was quick to see the faults in everyone else, but blind to any of his own.

Finally, his father looked at him and said, "Son, give me the bracelet. It's not making you like Jesus! Jesus said He didn't come to condemn the world but to save the world." Brian went on to explain that trying to follow Jesus's example was too much for any five-year-old or his family to handle. WWJD was a harder law than even the Ten Commandments, and men couldn't live up to those commandments of God, so Jesus came and lived them for us. Then He died in our place so all His righteousness could live in us. Jesus lives in us and works through us to become like Him. This is grace working from the inside out, not the law trying to work itself into our hearts.

Perhaps you've had one of those bracelets resting invisibly around your wrist. Have you been trying to be like Jesus, rather than to simply let His grace live in you? If so, you're either under much condemnation or in a state of blind conceit. Either way, there is only one—and will forever only be one—Champion. Jesus is the great Champion. Only as we let the life of Jesus work in us will His grace be released to make us more like Him. Becoming like Jesus doesn't happen by conscious effort, but rather by constant consideration of the grace of our Champion, Jesus Christ.

Jesus is the Champion of Grace we desire. He is the Champion of Grace we desperately need. He is the Champion we don't deserve. He is the Champion of Grace who willingly avails Himself to us, if we will only enlist in His battle for grace!

Are you ready to enlist? Are you ready to make Jesus your Champion? Are you willing to be His disciple? Are you ready to marvel at His gracious words? Are you ready to receive the abundance of grace He's won for you?

....

Lord, You are the ultimate champion. You are the One our hearts desperately long for. You are everything we need. You are good. You are kind. You are faithful. You are strong. You are wise. You are invincible. You are gracious. Work in my heart to accept Your grace in choosing me. Open my ears to hear Your gracious words. Open my eyes to behold the grace You exemplified in Your interactions with men, women, multitudes, and even Your enemies. Let the power of Your grace in Your suffering, Your crucifixion, and Your resurrection minister to my heart. Be my Champion forever and ever! In the name of the great Champion of Grace, Jesus, I ask these things. Amen!

For consideration:

1. What do you long for in a hero? How does Jesus embody those deepest desires?
2. What aspect of Jesus's grace ministers to you from
   - the disciples?
     * Which disciple do you think you're the most like?
     * How does Jesus's choosing of that disciple enrich your appreciation of grace?
   - sinners?
   - His enemies?

- His suffering?
- His resurrection?

3. List any misconceptions you've held about Jesus's grace.

4. What does the word *champion* convey to you about Jesus?

5. Why is trying to simply live like Jesus dangerous?

Eight

Enlisted in Grace

*I know that You are a gracious and merciful God, slow to anger and
abundant in lovingkindness, One who relents from doing harm.*

JONAH 4:2

Although in some countries military service is compulsory for
every young man and woman between the ages of 18 and 25,
currently young people join the U.S. military only by enlisting. Yet
when I was a young girl, the U.S. draft—a way of conscripting men
into military service since the Civil War—was still in force. Regardless of their opinion concerning the war's cause, men in that time
were recruited, trained, placed in a platoon, and sent into battle.

The draft was employed as a means of recruitment during both
World Wars, as well as for the conflicts in Korea and Vietnam. Married or not, men of age were required to register for service, and
they could be called to duty at a moment's notice. As an incentive
to enlistment, those men who voluntarily signed up were allowed to
choose the branch of the military they would serve in and commissioned to better posts, but anyone who illegally avoided their duty
to serve in the armed forces was considered a "draft dodger."

In 1968 Richard Nixon ran for president of the United States on the platform of ending the draft. He believed an army made up of soldiers who believed in the cause of the conflict and voluntarily enlisted in the service would make for a better and stronger military.

In 1971 the draft was officially put to rest. To this day, however, men are still required by law to register with the Selective Service System when they're 18 and to be ready to defend the United States of America.

As a member of God's kingdom, grace is not always a voluntary enlistment. God will often draft us into His service of grace. He will commission us to grace, press us to grace, minister grace through us, reveal the power of grace to us, and all the while teach us lessons about His great grace.

The Grace Call (Jonah 1:1-5)

The Bible's book of Jonah begins with God's call to the prophet Jonah. Jonah was from the town of Gath in Israel, and he had come to prominence because of the fulfillment of a prophecy he'd announced to the nation. Though the king of Israel, Jeroboam, was wicked in the eyes of the Lord, he nevertheless had reigned over the land prosperously for 41 years. Second Kings 14:25 tells us, "[Jeroboam] restored the territory of Israel from the entrance of Hamath to the Sea of Arabah, according to the word of the LORD God of Israel, which He had spoken through His servant Jonah the son of Amittai, the prophet who was from Gath Hepher." No doubt this positive word from the Lord put Jonah in good standing with the Israelites.

The nation had a dreaded enemy at the time—the Assyrians. They were known for the cruelty they inflicted on their adversaries. Uncovered in archaeological digs are reliefs depicting gruesome punishments meted out to their enemies. Among those ghastly scenes are beheadings and burnings. The capital of the barbaric Assyrian Empire was Nineveh.

Imagine Jonah's dismay when the word of the Lord came to him. God's previous message to Jonah had concerned the prosperity of Israel. This new message had to do with warning the city of Nineveh against divine judgment. God said to Jonah, "'Arise, go to Nineveh, that great city, and cry out against it; for their wickedness has come up before Me'" (1:2).

The good works of Nineveh's citizens didn't come up before God, nor their sorrow, innocence, or even their ignorance. No! It was their wickedness. No redeemable quality existed in Nineveh to merit the grace of God. The draw was their wickedness. Here were a people utterly set for destruction. They needed to know the saving grace of God.

Jonah, as a patriot of Israel, didn't want Nineveh saved. He wanted God to destroy it. Have you ever felt that way about your enemies? If so, then you understand how Jonah must have felt. The Assyrians were a constant threat to Israel. They were always conspiring to invade, conquer, and pillage the land of Jonah's people.

Jonah thought he could run from this commission. You might think of him as the original draft dodger. Reaching Nineveh required a journey over land, traveling northeast of Israel. Jonah went in the opposite direction and by the opposite means. The reluctant prophet went west, to the port of Joppa. There he purchased passage on a boat heading toward Tarshish, which was about as far away as anyone could get from Nineveh. (Most scholars believe Tarshish was an ancient port on the coast of Spain.)

Jonah sought lodging in the lowest part of the ship, believing he could hide from God's call in its hold. But no sooner was the vessel out to sea than "the Lord sent out a great wind" and "a mighty tempest" arose (1:4). As the sailors on the ship struggled to save it, Jonah slept, unaware of the danger his behavior had foisted on the crew.

Jonah's refusal to heed the grace call had incurred the wrath of God. Wrath is the actual consequence of disobeying God's law. The wrath Jonah wanted to descend on his enemies was now in full fury against the very men who were trying to save him and the ship by jettisoning cargo and expending all their energies.

Refusing the call to grace always presents a danger. God is determined to call us to grace, and He is committed to using whatever means necessary to cause us to embrace His call. When we refuse grace, however, the same oblivion that encapsulated Jonah encapsulates our minds and hearts. We, like Jonah, sleep because we fail to realize we've been sustained by God's grace our whole lives. We sleep because we don't realize how dangerous and desperate a life devoid of divine grace is. We sleep because we don't realize a refusal of God's grace is a choice for God's wrath. This is the perilous sleep of ignorance, and there can be no grace for others until we recognize how destitute we ourselves are without it. While we sleep, the lives of others are imperiled.

In 1850, Hudson Taylor, a young medical student in England, heard the call to grace. His mind and spirit were suddenly awakened by the knowledge that hundreds of men and women were perishing in China without the gospel. In 1853, he postponed his education and traveled to China, where he chose to live as the Chinese people lived. He dressed as they dressed, learned to speak Chinese, and lived among them. Later he returned to England to convince other young men and women to take the gospel of grace to China. He said, "Can all the Christians in England sit still with folded arms while these multitudes are perishing—perishing for lack of knowledge—for lack of knowledge which England possesses so richly?"[1]

God's grace awakened Hudson Taylor to the peril of those without Christ. He was stirred by the thought of men and women fighting the storms of life without knowing the God of All Grace.

I know many people who would rather sleep and leave men and women to perish in unbelief because they're more concerned for their personal comfort than for the salvation of others. They're the ultimate nationals and patriots of their self-cause. They condemn the very mission field God has placed them in.

This was not the case for my husband's dear friend Al Braca. Al was a loving, gracious, and outspoken Christian. Everyone at his workplace knew how important his faith was to him, but some of them were determined to undermine and mock his faith. It wasn't uncommon for Al to turn on his computer and find someone had posted a pornographic image. These same persecutors loved to watch his face when they told a dirty joke. Al found it hard to "love your enemies" and to "do good to those who hate you" (Matthew 5:44).

One day before leaving for work, Al asked his wife, Jean, to pray with him. "God has shown me my work is my mission field," he told her, "so we need to pray together before I go out that door." From that day forward Jean and Al got on their knees every morning and prayed for Al's company, for his coworkers, and for Al to be able to manifest God's grace to others. It worked! God gave him an extra portion of grace to endure his coworkers' barbs and consistently shower them with kindness.

Soon Al was calling Jean from work on a weekly basis to say he would be home late because he needed to minister to someone at work. Al became the go-to guy at the office when someone was in turmoil. Al listened. Al cared. Al prayed.

Al worked for a company in New York City with offices in the Twin Towers. On the morning of September 11, 2001, he and Jean prayed together, and then Al went to work and sat down at his desk in the North Tower. Soon the building was rocked by the force of a Boeing 767-223ER when it crashed into it ten floors below, killing all 92 people aboard. Realizing death was inevitable, Al's coworkers rushed to him. He directed them to join hands then he explained the reality of heaven and how by the grace of God through Jesus Christ, they could all accompany him there that day. Then Al led the whole assembly in a prayer before the North Tower gave way and crumbled to the ground.

For days after the towers collapsed, Al's wife received phone calls from relatives of those who had died with Al. They read a variety of texts and related the last phone conversations they had with their loved ones, explaining what Al had done. One of the most notable texts said, "Going to heaven with Al Braca."

What if Al had been numb to the peril of his coworkers that day? What if he had viewed them as enemies rather than potential recipients of God's grace? A whole company of individuals in heaven is now sitting with Abraham, Isaac, and Jacob. If asked how they got there, they'll answer, "With Al Braca, of course!"

Exposed! (Jonah 1:6-16)

One of the worst Christian witnesses is graceless behavior. Nothing is more humiliating than to act in a graceless manner, only to have it discovered you're a Christian!

My father, a pastor, loved to tell the story about a woman in front of him at the grocery store. She was yelling at the checkout clerk over some perceived mistake. The clerk was calm and absorbing the fury, but the woman continued by showering the hapless employee with a variety of expletives. Then she turned to pour a bit of her rage on the people behind her in line. That's when she saw my dad. "Chuck!" she cried with an element of surprise and shame commingling.

Dad gave her one of his brilliant smiles. "Hello there. Sounds like you're having a pretty bad day. Like you need to make sure you don't miss next Sunday's message about loving one another." The woman tried to stammer some excuse as she gathered her groceries, and then she fled the store.

The captain of the ship found Jonah fast asleep while his men were desperately fighting the violent storm and praying to their pagan gods for help. Jonah was brought to the deck, where because they recognized a spiritual force behind the terrible tempest, the hardened mariners were trying to determine the spiritual cause of the storm. They cast lots to see who was to blame for such a catastrophe. The lot fell on Jonah.

Immediately, the men began to question him: "'Please tell us! For whose cause is this trouble upon us? What is your occupation? And where do you come from? What is your country? Of what people are you?'" (1:8).

Jonah had to admit, "'I am a Hebrew; and I fear the LORD, the God of heaven, who made the sea and the dry land'" (1:9). Jonah was confessing to these men that his God was the One who had power over the storm. The storm was happening because Jonah had tried to hide from the Lord. The men were beyond afraid and asked Jonah why he would do such a thing! Why would he run away and try to hide from such a powerful God?

Here's the factual answer Jonah probably didn't give: "I ran because I have no grace for people like you. I care more about my own comforts and my own people than I do about the people who are perishing because they don't know the living God of Israel."

No, I don't think Jonah confessed everything, because when he told these men the way to stop the storm was to throw him overboard, they were reluctant to do it. If they had known his true motivation, they might have been less reluctant!

The seamen made one last effort to save the ship. Then having exhausted every other method, they prayed to the Lord, "'Please do not let us perish for this man's life, and do not charge us with innocent blood; for You, O Lord, have done as it pleased You'" (1:14). Having made their peace with God, they threw Jonah into the raging sea, and immediately the storm stopped!

Grace is one of the best ways to avoid humiliation. Proverbs 3:34 states, "Surely He scorns the scornful, but gives grace to the humble." Jonah's scorn for his enemies brought the scorn of the seamen, and Jonah was found out.

He was caught sleeping.

He was caught numb and ignorant to the peril of others.

He was caught as a "draft dodger"—running from God's call.

He was caught as the one who had jeopardized the ship and crew.

He was caught as a hypocrite, the disobedient prophet of God who told others to obey God while he disobeyed Him.

Another Proverb states, "A gracious woman retains honor" (Proverbs 11:16). Conversely, a woman who doesn't act graciously won't retain honor. Graceless behavior will always lead to humiliation.

The men on the ship came to know the living God despite Jonah's graceless behavior. Only through his humiliating confession, however, did these men learn the true cause of their peril and the lifesaving power of the God of the Hebrews.

Grace the Hard Way (Jonah 1:17–2:10)

God's chastening is often His way of teaching the greatest lessons of grace. Hebrews 12:10-11 says, "[Our fathers] indeed for a few days chastened us as seemed best to them, but [God] for our profit, that we may be partakers of His holiness. Now no chastening seems to be joyful for the present, but painful; nevertheless, afterward it yields the peaceable fruit of righteousness to those who have been trained by it." Chastening is part of God's grace. God refused to let Jonah go. He pursued Jonah. He continued to work with Jonah. He allowed Jonah to suffer the hard way so he could learn vital lessons about His grace.

The prophet didn't perish in the raging sea, though, because "the LORD had prepared a great fish to swallow Jonah" (1:17). That might not seem like a mercy to you, but God loved this wayward prophet, and He was thinking of his welfare. Jonah was developing some bad patterns in his life. As a prophet, he had the privilege of hearing God's word and sharing it with people. Yet Jonah thought he could ignore the word of God he didn't want to hear. He thought he could choose where and when not to obey God. He thought he could continue to harbor hatred in his heart, even when God was calling him to grace. These would be dangerous patterns in anyone's life, but they were lethal to someone representing the God of Israel!

The "great fish" spared Jonah's life. Jonah spent a miserable three days and three nights in the hot moisture of its belly, a type of hell for the prophet. It was a foretaste of where those who refuse God's saving grace would end up. As he prayed to the Lord, Jonah testified, "'The floods surrounded me; all Your billows and Your waves passed over me... The waters surrounded me, even to my soul; the deep closed around me; weeds were wrapped around my head. I went down to the moorings of the mountains; the earth with its bars closed behind me forever'" (2:3-6).

Let's imagine his experience. He was cramped. Gastric juices enveloped him. The stench of the belly fluids nauseated him. He felt every plunge, turn, and movement of the fish. Seaweed constricted his whole body. He was trapped in a stinky, watery, acidic, confining, and swirling dungeon.

Is this the type of place you want others to go to? When I experience something miserable, I warn others—even people I don't know.

Before this experience, Jonah was callous and indifferent to the eternal destiny of others.

Jonah prayed and was heard by God even from the depths of the ocean floor. Now, that's grace! God not only heard Jonah's prayer, but He regarded the prayer of the disobedient prophet.

Jonah recognized his folly. He said, "'Those who regard worthless idols forsake their own Mercy'" (2:8). The Hebrew word used here for idol is *hebel*. A better translation is "vanity" or "lies." In other words, Jonah realized he'd believed worthless lies. He'd believed he could disobey God successfully. He'd believed he could refuse the call of God. He'd believed he could run from God. He'd believed he could hide from God. In running and trying to hide, he had forsaken his own mercy, or to state it plainly, he'd brought all this trouble on himself.

Jonah vowed to sacrifice to God. He vowed to obey God. He would relinquish his comforts, his way, and his self-will to God. Now, mind you, he did promise this while he was in the belly of the fish. I've seen people promise to obey God when the consequences of their bad choices begin to close in on them. Many times, however, these people go right back to their worthless idols as soon as the pressure is off.

God spoke to the fish, and it heaved Jonah onto dry ground.

This isn't the way I want to learn grace. What about you? Yet the Lord will at times give us a foretaste of the misery of sin and sinners so we'll have greater grace. It's been said that earth is the closest a Christian will ever be to hell but also the closest an unbeliever will ever be to heaven. That's a sobering thought that should motivate us to grace.

I've heard Christians too easily condemn people to hell. Anyone who claims to know Jesus and can blithely do that should be looking over their shoulder for a "great fish."

God wanted to show Jonah the expedience of grace. For three days and three nights, he experienced life without grace. It was a hard lesson, but so necessary. God wants to teach you the glory of grace. He wants you to have His heart of grace. He's the One who looked down on the rebellious earth and "so loved the world that He gave His only begotten Son, that whoever believes in Him should not perish but have everlasting life" (John 3:16).

Second-Chance Grace (Jonah 3)

A speaker I once heard said, "God is the God of the second, third, fourth, and billionth chance." God's grace continues to be extended to everyone throughout the duration of their lives. This truth was brought home to me when I interviewed a young pastor's wife. She and her husband have a thriving ministry, and I asked how she came to know the Lord.

She told me she was brought up in a tumultuous home. Her mother and father regularly indulged in hard drugs, and the family experienced constant violence until her father left home. Then her mother took up with one drug-addicted boyfriend after another. The young woman I interviewed left home at an early age. By her late teens she was an unwed mother, a prostitute, and looking at some serious jail time.

In prison she gave her life to the Lord. Once back out on the streets, however, she retracted the commitment she made, and it wasn't long until she was back in prison. Again, she made a commitment to the Lord. This commitment was a bit stronger, as was her sentence. She dedicated her time behind bars to Bible study, prayer, and growing in the Lord. Before her release, she was warned to abandon her old boyfriend and give her all to Jesus.

Yet once out, within days she'd taken up with her old boyfriend. For a time they went to church and studied the Word together, but then they began to fall back into old patterns and both were incarcerated.

Back for the third time, she thoroughly repented. She promised to give God everything regardless of the difficulties ahead. Again, she was released, and again she committed herself to Bible study and fellowship, but also to accountability. So did her old boyfriend. They tried to ignore their attraction to each other, but they couldn't and decided to get married. Knowing their past history and weaknesses, they prayed for more grace and more strength to grow in the Lord. They both attended Bible college and graduated. Within a few years, he was offered the pastorate of a small church in a bad part of town. After talking with his wife and much prayer, he accepted the commission with grace. They're still there, and God has used them to minister to countless lives just like theirs. Why? Because God is the God of the second, third, fourth, and a billion chances.

As we pick up the story of Jonah, the word of the Lord comes to him a second time. God gives him the same commission He'd given him before the whale ride: "'Arise, go to Nineveh, that great city, and preach to it the message that I tell you'" (3:2). This time "Jonah arose and went to Nineveh" (3:3).

The ruins of the ancient city of Nineveh were uncovered by Sir Austen Layard in the nineteenth century. Since that time the site has been extensively excavated, and what these archaeologists uncovered is extraordinary! Nineveh was a walled city about a mile and a half wide and approximately three miles long. One of its longer walls ran parallel with the Tigris River. The walls surrounding Nineveh were 40 to 50 feet high and stretched eight miles around the inner city. The city contained its own water system with one of the oldest aqueducts in history. Unearthed was a 71-room palace with walls of sculptured slabs. A library housed more than 22,000 clay tablets. The city contained many temples to the pagan gods they worshiped.

It took Jonah three days to walk through that entire city. When he entered it on the first day, he began to cry out, "'Yet forty days, and Nineveh shall be overthrown'" (3:4).

The people believed Jonah and the message from God. They proclaimed a fast, and all the residents, from the least to the greatest, put on mourning clothes. When word of Jonah's message reached the king, he laid aside his royal robes, donned mourning garments as well, and issued an edict that was proclaimed throughout the city:

> Let neither man nor beast, herd nor flock, taste anything; do not let them eat, or drink water. But let man and beast be covered with sackcloth, and cry mightily to God; yes, let every one turn from his evil way and from the violence that is in his hands. Who can tell if God will turn and relent, and turn away from His fierce anger, so that we may not perish? (3:7-9).

Now that's repentance! That's one successful evangelistic endeavor!

God's grace poured over Nineveh when He saw their works and how they had turned from their evil ways. Nineveh did what the nation of Israel refused to do—they heeded the word of the prophet. How gracious of God to forgive Jonah, chasten Jonah, reinstate His call to Jonah, and bless Jonah's mission.

God has a grace call for all of us. He desires to use us as ministers and dispensers of His grace. As He did with Jonah, He will constrain us by whatever means necessary to bring us into that call.

God's call always contains God's purpose. He doesn't call us in vain, but into the work He plans to do. Through His call He allows us to be partakers in His grace.

Even when we refuse, try to run away, and reject the call of God, He doesn't refuse, run away from, or reject us. He continues to hunt us down with His grace, and when we're ready, He calls us again into His purposes.

Another Lesson in Grace (Jonah 4)

You would think the prophet would be overjoyed by the repentance of Nineveh. This was greater success than any of the prophets in Israel had obtained. The Ninevites believed the word of God through Jonah and repented and turned from their evil ways. But Jonah wasn't happy about that! Jonah 4:1 records that "it displeased Jonah exceedingly, and he became angry." He *resented* the grace of God.

Some people don't want God's grace extended to others. I'd like to say I don't understand that attitude, but I do. For a time, in my heart I had a collection of people I felt deserved the grace of God. Outside that "grace club," however, were those people I didn't want to receive good things from God. I didn't necessarily want them punished; I just didn't want them blessed by God's grace. How's that for a misunderstanding of grace?

It all came to a head one day, when I, the president of the grace club, violated every ordinance and principle I had set up. It was a bad day—one of my worst days yet. I had to resign from the presidency and membership of my own grace club, or more accurately, I was kicked out.

I remember blubbering before the Lord that day. I was shocked at my own behavior. I was so angry with myself. I really had expected better things of the president of the grace club. But God spoke to me so gently, and I still remember the sweet impression He left on my heart: *Cheryl, I never liked your grace club. I never joined it. I'm glad it's over. Grace isn't for just a few deserving people. By its very nature, grace is for all those who don't deserve it, so here's some grace for you.*

God forgave me and disbanded the grace club forever in my heart!

So, yes, I understand Jonah's attitude. I've had some of those feelings myself. Ugh. Jonah didn't want the Ninevites spared, let alone repentant, saved, and shown mercy. He wanted to see them judged for all their past cruelties to Israel.

Can you imagine saying to God, "I told You so!" That seems like the height of arrogance, and yet that's exactly what Jonah did, though not in so many words: "'Ah, LORD, was not this what I said when I was still in my country? Therefore I fled previously to Tarshish; for I know that You are a gracious and merciful God, slow to anger and abundant in lovingkindness, One who relents from doing harm'" (4:2).

Rather than appreciating and embracing the grace of God, Jonah was angry. It seems like he had developed his own grace club. He wanted God's grace extended toward him and Israel, but not toward the Ninevites. That's what I call selective grace. I've met believers like that. They claim to know the God of All Grace and are recipients of that divine grace, but they don't like seeing God show grace to others! They have a list of stipulations and regulations about to whom God should and should not show grace.

Jonah resented God's grace toward Nineveh, and he was so angry he wanted to die: "'Therefore now, O LORD, please take my life from me, for it is better for me to die than to live!'" (4:3). That's a strong reaction! Yet observe God's grace toward Jonah. Jonah's prayer is like a backward compliment. On the one hand he's justifying his disobedience in fleeing to Tarshish, and at the same time he's angry with God for His grace, mercy, and lovingkindness! What grace for God to allow the prophet to talk to Him in this manner. If God were not gracious, merciful, and full of lovingkindness, Jonah's prayer would have toasted him!

On a side note, isn't it wondrous how honest we can be with God? He doesn't want our false affections; He wants authenticity.

Our God desires "truth in the inward parts" (Psalm 51:6). In His grace, He receives our honest prayers, even when we're angry and confused, have the facts wrong, or are demanding the wrong things. By His grace, God is able to hear, amend, purify, and answer our prayers with the perfect response.

God asks Jonah, "'Is it right for you to be angry?'" (4:4). God is about to teach this angry prophet one more lesson about grace.

Jonah goes outside the city and camps on the east side. The prophet is still hoping for judgment, and this is an unhealthy place to be camped. I've known people preoccupied and even obsessed with the judgment of others. They tend to camp at a certain place spiritually, emotionally, and mentally, and they can't be moved. Their minds and hearts are always focused on judgment. And when judgment tarries or isn't carried out, they, like Jonah, are miserable and angry with God.

Even as the Lord prepared a great fish to teach Jonah a lesson in grace, He prepared a plant, a worm, and an east wind for Jonah's final lesson. It's almost like a flannelgraph lesson. God uses these unusual elements to teach the angry prophet about His gentleness, kindness, and mercy.

As Jonah sat on the outskirts of Nineveh, God prepared a plant to spring up and bring some shade to Jonah from the merciless heat. Jonah was grateful for the plant. The next morning, however, God prepared a worm to damage the plant so it would wither. Jonah not only lost his only source of shade, but God prepared an aggressively strong and hot east wind to beat on Jonah's head. Jonah was so miserable in that graceless place he wished for death. "'It is better for me to die than to live!'" he said (4:3).

Again, God was bringing Jonah to the place of grace. It took absolute misery for Jonah to appreciate and embrace God's grace. It took discomfort and the misery of being in a grace-forsaken place for him to recognize the necessity and mercy of grace.

God asked the prophet a second time, "'Is it right for you to be angry?'"—this time about the plant (4:9). Jonah again justified himself. "'It is right for me to be angry, even to death!'" (4:9). That's some attitude!

The plant provided shade for Jonah, so Jonah received the plant into the grace club. For Jonah, grace was to be extended only to those people and things that added to his comfort. He thought his perception of grace was acceptable. It was not, and God wanted Jonah to understand the depths of His grace. Jonah had pity for a plant whose duration was short-lived. However, he had no grace or pity for the 120,000 people in Nineveh who could "not discern between their right hand and their left" (4:11). God had compassion on these people, and He wanted His prophet to share His affection.

We're not specifically told in Scripture, but something must have dawned in Jonah's heart. No doubt he wrote down this tremendous lesson of grace to share it with the people of Israel when he returned to his homeland.

Are you ready to enlist in the battle of grace? Are you ready to disband your "grace club" to see the lost and undeserving receiving the grace of God? God is calling you into His service of grace. Are you going to go voluntarily? Or will you have to be conscripted into the reserves of His grace?

....

Lord, I find my own testimony in the life of Jonah. You know the times I've tried to hide and run away from Your call of grace. I pray that You'll forgive me. Grace is so important to You. It's a part of Your nature. You are gracious. You are merciful. You are abundant in lovingkindness. You want to manifest Your grace to the world, and You desire to call me into this grace service with You. Teach me the riches of Your grace. Give me an appreciation of Your grace. Help me embrace Your grace. Grant me the grace to forgive my enemies and seek to see them receive Your grace. I want to enlist in Your army of grace. I want to be an ally of grace. In the name of Jesus, who brought Your grace to all mankind, amen.

For consideration:

1. With which of these ways can you relate to Jonah's life?

   - trying to hide from God's call

   - running from God's call

   - chastening

   - second chances

   - learning the lesson of grace

2. Compare Jonah's experience in the belly of the great fish (Jonah 2:2-6) with Jesus's description of hell in Mark 9:48. Why should Christians not be quick to pray for judgment?

3. What lessons do you observe about grace from Jonah's life?

4. What is your lasting impression about God's grace toward Nineveh?

Nine

Use It or Lose It

He said to me, "My grace is sufficient for you, for My strength is made perfect in weakness." Therefore most gladly I will rather boast in my infirmities, that the power of Christ may rest upon me.

2 CORINTHIANS 12:9

One of the most colorful missionaries to China has got to be Gladys Aylward. Her story, found in the book *The Little Woman*, is one of my favorite missionary stories.[1] Gladys was born on February 12, 1902, in Edmonton, London, England, and since in those days domestic service was about the only future prospect a young girl from an ordinary family had there, that was how she eventually supported herself.

Gladys had grown up in a churchgoing home, but she was more of a cultural Christian. Then one night she went to a meeting where the gospel was presented, and suddenly Gladys understood the work of Jesus as she never had before. She realized He had a claim on her life, and she dedicated her life to the Lord that night.

As she was reading a Christian magazine just a few months later, an article about China deeply moved her. She talked to her friends about possibly going there as a missionary. They encouraged her to continue in domestic service as a maid and use her earnings to help financially support the missionaries already stationed in China. This didn't settle right with Gladys, and the desire to go to China kept increasing.

Eventually Gladys applied to a missions board. After testing her, they concluded she didn't have the aptitude and vitality to be a missionary to China. They felt at her age and with her limited intellectual prowess she wouldn't be able to learn the complicated Chinese language.

Gladys sought the Lord, and rather than her determination to go to China dampening, it was confirmed. She went to a local travel agency and put a down payment on the cheapest one-way ticket to China available. From her limited funds working as a parlor maid, Gladys made weekly installments on her ticket.

Gladys had no idea what she would do in China since she didn't speak Chinese, but she avidly read any books she found on the culture and learned a few phrases. One day a friend of her employer told her about a widow, Mrs. Lawson, who was serving in China. Jeannie Lawson was 73 and praying for someone younger to come to China and carry on the ministry she administered. Gladys immediately wrote to Mrs. Lawson and explained her desire, her endeavors, and her willingness to come. After some time, the reply came all the way from China to Gladys's front door. It was succinct: If Gladys could come to Tientsin, Jeannie Lawson would meet her there. Gladys packed her bags.

The story of Gladys's passage is harrowing and packed with miracles, but when she finally reached Tientsin, a Mr. Lu escorted her the many miles to Yangchen, where Jeannie Lawson owned and operated the Inn of Sixth Happiness. Mrs. Lawson immediately put Gladys to work.

The Inn of Sixth Happiness was on the trade route, and traveling merchants stayed there. Inside the inn was a large courtyard with a fire burning for warmth. The horses and other pack animals were fed, housed, and protected while the merchants were told Bible stories in the Chinese language as they ate and rested.

Gladys's first job was to use phrases Jeannie taught her to go out into the streets and compel merchants to come to the inn. Gladys did her job with gusto, often grabbing mules by the harness and coaxing whole caravans to seek their lodging at the Inn of Sixth Happiness. The merchants were engrossed in Mrs. Lawson's Bible stories and often responded to the message of God's Son coming to earth to live and die for their sins. These merchants then went to the different villages throughout the province, telling others about the Inn of Sixth Happiness and the wondrous stories they'd heard there.

Gladys memorized the stories Jeannie Lawson repeated each night before the roaring fire. She practiced them again and again, using the same inflections she'd heard from the aged missionary. Jeannie soon had Gladys sharing the stories with the traveling merchants.

With Jeannie's health deteriorating quickly, more and more duties and responsibilities were relegated to Gladys until she was the one running the Inn of Sixth Happiness. When Jeannie Lawson died, Gladys simply kept doing what she'd been doing.

Gladys practiced and used the Chinese she'd learned over and over until she became proficient in the language. It soon became so natural to her that she thought as well as spoke it. This proficiency unexpectedly opened many doors and offered a myriad of miraculous opportunities for Gladys to share the gospel. She became one of the most effective missionaries to ever enter China.

It's important to note that Gladys became proficient in the Chinese language because she practiced and incorporated it into every aspect of her life. She didn't just memorize certain phrases; she applied them to all she did until she was even thinking in Chinese.

Practicing Grace

In the same way, grace must be practiced until we're proficient in it. We can't just assume certain aspects of grace; we must receive grace into our hearts and let it inundate our entire being so we begin to think gracious thoughts and operate in grace. Proverbs 16:3 states, "Commit your works to the LORD, and your thoughts will be established." When we desire to be gracious, our thoughts become established in grace. To really learn, think, and operate in grace, we need to begin to apply grace to every aspect of our lives.

As women engaged in the battle for grace, we must learn to use the implements and power of grace. We must become skilled and practiced in grace.

Paul was an apostle who learned the power of grace firsthand. He was a fierce opponent of the gospel of grace until he had a personal encounter with the God of All Grace. Before this encounter, Saul—Paul's name until the Lord changed it—hunted down Christians and arrested them. He was violent in his dealings. He would burst into households and drag whole families to prison. In his misguided zeal for God and the Mosaic Law, he was vehement, aggressive, and cruel.

Then one day—the day he met Jesus—his whole life was drastically altered.

Saul had heard the church was growing in Damascus. He received an official injunction from the high priest to go there, hunt down the believers, and bring them back to Jerusalem to be tried. Accompanied by a band of like-minded men, Saul set out on his mission. On the road at noontime, however, a great light blinded the persecutor and propelled him to his knees. Then a rumbling voice sounded from heaven: "'Saul, Saul, why are you persecuting Me?'" (Acts 9:4).

Shaken, Saul asked, "'Who are You, Lord?'" (verse 5). Already his bravado was melting. He was ready to serve this new Sovereign who had arrested him on his mission. The voice answered, "'I am Jesus, who you are persecuting. It is hard for you to kick against the goads'" (verse 5).

Can you imagine this encounter? The very person Saul had been aggressively sinning against was present and powerfully calling him to account for everything he'd done. Jesus was not only alive; He was powerful! Saul trembled as he meekly asked, "'Lord, what do You want me to do?'" (verse 6).

I wonder what he expected. Having fought so hard and cruelly against the people of Jesus, he must have expected to receive the same harshness and cruelty. The trials of the Sanhedrin were brutal and ended in condemnation. Saul was on trial here. Yet the word of the Lord was, "'Arise, and go into the city, and you will be told what you must do'" (verse 6).

From that day forward Saul became Paul, the apostle of Jesus Christ. With the utmost dedication to Jesus Christ, Paul heralded the gospel, sought to persuade men to know Jesus, taught in synagogues and churches, traveled throughout the empire of Rome as the first missionary of the gospel, wrote doctrinal and instructional letters to the churches, endured riots and persecutions, and established churches in many of the major cities of the empire. Though Paul endured persecution, he was greatly used by God, and the church flourished under his ministry.

Paul credited God's grace as the reason for all his success. He'd met grace on the road to Damascus. Jesus, in His grace, sought out Paul. Paul was on the road to destruction when Jesus forcefully stopped him in his tracks and then revealed His power to him. Yet Paul needed to learn even more grace.

I think Paul was a can-do type of guy. Give him a job and he'd throw all his considerable energy, strength, and time into it. Before he met Jesus, he had already gained the position of a Pharisee. He was educated beyond his peers. He was zealous in his dedication and service to the Mosaic Law. However, service to Jesus Christ would require divine energy, strength, and power. Paul learned the secret of this power when he ran out of his own reserves of endurance.

Paul had an affliction so severe that he described it as "a messenger of Satan" buffeting him (2 Corinthians 12:7). Three times he implored the Lord to take away the infirmity. Paul, no doubt, felt that without the setback of suffering, he could serve the Lord more effectively.

Paul was a man of prayer. He sought the Lord daily. I think this "thorn in the flesh" was often a subject of prayer. On three specific occasions, however, it became more than the apostle could bear. On those occasions he pleaded with the Lord to take it away (2 Corinthians 12:7-9).

God's response to Paul was revolutionary to the apostle. Though he had received God's saving grace and was called by God's grace into divine service, Paul was to learn to implement this same grace in every endeavor, deficiency, and circumstance. God said to him, "'My grace is sufficient for you, for My strength is made perfect in weakness'" (verse 9). This answer was unexpected and revelatory. God was showing Paul a superior means to life and ministry—the means of grace.

Like the apostle, we all have places in our lives we want to pray away. Often we think, *If I just didn't have this or that, I could serve the Lord more effectively. If I just didn't have*

> *this job.*
> *this family member.*
> *this location.*
> *this illness.*
> *this weakness.*
> *this person in my life.*
> *this culture.*
> *this limitation.*
> *this history.*
> *this bill.*
> *this responsibility.*
> *this pain.*
> *this deficit.*

I've even said to the Lord in prayer, "If You would just remove this from my life, I could be so much more effective for You." We fail to realize that God allows these very issues into our lives purposefully, even artfully, to constrain us to the greater power of His grace.

I remember years ago saying to the Lord, "If I didn't have this nose and these keen olfactory senses, I could be so much more effective in my service for You!" Unfortunately, I was born with a keen ability to smell. I can sniff out any odor. To me it often seemed like a curse. I'm easily nauseated and literally sickened by smells. My nose has greatly limited my job opportunities, places of ministry, and to whom I can minister.

One year when I was overseeing a women's retreat in the countryside of England, a certain woman came. Hannah had never been to a retreat. For years she'd been housebound because of the humiliation of a skin disease that covered her body. She registered by phone, and I and those working with me were overjoyed at the opportunity to love on Hannah.

Hannah had a vibrant personality, and though she was self-conscious about her disfigurement, others at the retreat were most conscious of her smell. The odor was so bad that though it was December and snowing outside, we kept the windows wide open in the meeting room. All the women wore their parkas to the services.

Hannah wanted a moment alone with me. We stood in the doorway to talk, and I found myself gagging. It was an involuntary response, and I was doing my best to suppress it. I tried to not breathe through my nose to counteract the effect Hannah's stench was having on me. When I tried to breathe through my mouth, however, I could almost taste the smell of dried urine and feces that emanated from her body. I had to make my excuses, turn away, and find a bathroom, where the contents of my stomach vacated my body.

I felt terrible! I wanted desperately to minister the love of God to Hannah. She was insecure, lonely, and feeling rejected. I prayed to the Lord to desensitize my olfactory nerves. It didn't happen, but a group of women discreetly asked me if something could be done about Hannah. They, like me, wanted to love on her, but the stench was nauseating them to the point of distraction from the Bible studies.

I went back to prayer. Rather than complaining about my nose, I asked for wisdom. Suddenly the idea was laid on my heart to go into town and buy Hannah all new clothes. I asked a friend to go with me. We found a clothing store, and before entering it, we prayed, "Lord, we don't know Hannah's size or what she needs. You love her, and we trust you to show us. We want Hannah, as Your child, to feel loved and wanted."

Inside the store we purchased undergarments, a shirt, a sweater, slacks, a scarf, a warm jacket, socks, and even shoes. We found all these items at greatly reduced prices. They were not only good-looking and practical, but bargains! God knew we were on a limited budget. Next, we hit the market, where we bought soap, shampoo, conditioner, deodorant, deodorant spray, face flannels (the English term for wash cloths), and a towel.

We were elated until we reached the conference center. Now a new dilemma presented itself. How were we to get the items to Hannah without offending her? Who would be willing to help Hannah bathe and use these items?

I asked a nurse at the conference if she would be willing. She flatly refused, and I couldn't fault her. After all, this wasn't something I wanted to or even felt capable of doing. Then I saw my friend Pam, who was visiting from California. I knew she had often volunteered with ministries to the homeless. Meekly, I approached her, holding the bags of newly purchased items. A smile lit up Pam's beautiful face. "I would love to," she said. Then her countenance slightly fell. "But" she added, "I wouldn't want to rob anyone else of the blessing." We assured her that no one else wanted that blessing.

Again, we prayed, and Pam took the bags to Hannah's room. Hannah was suspicious as she eyed Pam and the bags. Pam explained she was there because Jesus loved Hannah and had a gift for her. Hannah was still suspicious, but she let Pam into the room. "How does Jesus know what size I wear?" Pam prayed a quick prayer for wisdom before responding, "He knows you thoroughly. Let's see what He bought you."

Pam began to remove each item from the bag. Hannah's excitement grew as each new and beautiful item was displayed. Hannah agreed to a bath, but she admitted she hadn't had one in years because her skin disease had made them painful. Pam prayed with Hannah, and then Hannah allowed Pam to help her bathe. There was no pain, and now Hannah was clean. Tentatively, she put on the underwear and bra. They fit perfectly. Hannah began to jump up and down, chanting, "Jesus loves me, and He knows my size!"

Pam asked if she could spray the body deodorant on her. Hannah hesitated, and Pam sensed her apprehension. "Hannah, Jesus took the pain away when you bathed and gave you the perfect size underwear. Don't you think you can trust Him with this spray?" Hannah closed her eyes tight and braced for pain. "All right. Go ahead!"

Gently Pam began to mist Hannah's body. Hannah opened one eye and then the other. "There's no pain!" Hannah exclaimed. Then Pam went for it. She doused Hannah in the fragrant spray, and Hannah smelled wonderful!

Next came the shirt and slacks. Again, they were perfect fits. Then the sweater, hat, and scarf. Jesus had nailed it! Hannah put the socks on and then the shoes. Yep! Jesus knew her shoe size too. Finally, she tried on the jacket. Everything was just right!

When Hannah came to dinner that night, she had more invitations to sit at various tables than she knew what to do with. Later at service, people sat next to Hannah. She received more hugs at that retreat than she'd ever received in her life!

I had to ask myself, what if my nose hadn't been my deficit? Hannah would never have known the love of her sisters in Christ, and Pam would never have been able to minister to this precious sister in Christ.

Those things we wish we didn't have are often the very instruments God uses to lead us deeper into His grace. Conversely, even as we think we would be better *without* some things, we think we would be better *with* some things. The list can be extensive. We think, *I could serve God better if I had*

more money.

more energy.

more stamina.

more talent.

better health.

a better job.

better friends.

better opportunities.

better education.

better connections.

a better shape.

beauty.

prestige.

God replaces the unwanted elements of our lives as well as the deficits with His grace. Through and by the grace of Jesus, we have *all* we need. Again, 2 Corinthians 9:8 informs us that by grace we always have everything we need in abundance for everything God calls us to do! I know you read it already, but this passage bears repeating over and over until you know it by heart: "God is able to make all grace abound toward you, that you, always having all sufficiency in all things, may have an abundance for every good work."

It's important to note that this Scripture was written by the very apostle who learned to abound in the sufficiency of God's grace. In 2 Corinthians 12:10, Paul said that through God's grace he learned to "take pleasure in infirmities, in reproaches, in needs, in persecutions, in distresses, for Christ's sake." And then he said, "For when I am weak, then I am strong."

Paul learned the greatness of relying on God's grace. This grace takes away the limitations of our humanity and brings us into the realm of the divine. No longer does our time, talent, culture, intelligence, or education limit us, because grace compensates for every obstacle and deficit. By grace we can do what we've never been able to do before or have never felt capable of doing.

Like Paul, we must learn to rely on God's grace by drawing on it daily in a variety of ways. The more we begin to rely on God's grace above our own strength, the more our lives will take on a divinely spiritual demeanor.

The Blessing of Grace

One of the places we're to access grace is in blessing and being a blessing. When God established the order of the Aaronic priesthood, He instructed the priests to bless the people. What has come to be known as the Aaronic blessing is recorded in Numbers 6:24-26:

> "The LORD bless you and keep you;
> The LORD make His face shine upon you,
> And be gracious to you;
> The LORD lift up His countenance upon you,
> And give you peace."

God said this blessing of grace was how he would "put [His] name on the children of Israel" and "bless them" (Numbers 6:27).

We are to use God's grace to bless His people. Paul began every epistle he wrote with a greeting almost the same as "Grace to you and peace from God our Father and the Lord Jesus Christ" (Romans 1:7). He also ended every letter with a benediction of God's grace. I printed some references below you're welcome to look up or just observe to understand the importance of blessing others with God's grace.

Greeting	Benediction
Romans 1:7	Romans 16:24
Ephesians 1:2	Ephesians 6:24
Philippians 1:2	Philippians 4:23
Colossians 1:2	Colossians 4:18
1 Corinthians 1:3	1 Corinthians 16:23
2 Corinthians 1:2	2 Corinthians 13:14
Galatians 1:3	Galatians 6:18
1 Thessalonians 1:1	1 Thessalonians 5:28
2 Thessalonians 1:2	2 Thessalonians 3:18
1 Timothy 1:2	1 Timothy 6:21
2 Timothy 1:2	2 Timothy 4:22
Titus 1:4	Titus 3:15
Philemon 3	Philemon 25

We bless others with God's grace when we remind them of God's grace toward them and we pray God's grace over them.

In 1980, my dad heard someone sing the Aaronic blessing. He'd soon learned the song and began to teach it to the congregation at his church, Calvary Chapel. Then Dad, who ended every sermon with a blessing, began to implement the Aaronic blessing at the end of each service. After a benediction he would pray, and then he would sing the Aaronic blessing a cappella with the churchgoers singing along with him.

I was married in May 1980. My father chose to both walk me down the aisle and perform the ceremony. Then he and my mother commandeered my wedding plans. I wanted a small wedding at my brother's church. They wanted a large wedding at Calvary with the whole church invited. I chose and mailed invitations to select friends and family. My dad put an announcement in the church bulletin, inviting all the congregants to come. Brian and I chose a couple to sing our favorite songs at the wedding. Dad politely dismissed them and asked another man and young women to sing my mother's and his favorite songs from *Fiddler on the Roof.*

It might sound like they hijacked my wedding, and they did to a degree, but I was their youngest child and their last opportunity to have any input into one of their kids' wedding ceremonies. Brian adored my mom and dad and wasn't about to tell them no. So *Fiddler on the Roof* it was, and the whole church was invited. Two thousand people came on May 23 to watch Pastor Chuck's youngest daughter get married.

My mom and dad had one more surprise for us. Mom later told me Dad shared the idea with her, and when she agreed they were both excited about it. At the end of the wedding ceremony, when Brian and I turned to face the audience, Dad presented us as Mr. and Mrs. Brian Brodersen. Then as soon as the applause died down, he began to sing in his beautiful baritone voice, "The Lord bless thee, and keep thee…" The whole audience rose to their feet and began to sing it over us. It was awesome. It was a moment I'll never forget.

Just before my father died, I longed for him to bless me as Jacob in the Bible had blessed his sons. However, I never had the opportunity to voice my desire. Dad was so ill with cancer, but he kept trying to push through and minister to others. He just added a myriad of doctor appointments, radiation, and chemotherapy to his already brimming schedule. I didn't want to be one more demand on his life.

Then one Friday, after I'd taught the women's morning Bible study, I learned he'd been readmitted to the hospital for cellulitis. I picked up a hamburger for his private nurse and went straight to the hospital. My oldest brother was already there, as well as Dad's nurse. In the gentlest way possible, the doctor told my dad his body was riddled with cancerous tumors, and he gave him six weeks at the most to live. Dad was nonplussed at this news. He smiled at the doctor and thanked him. Then he asked him when he could eat again. The doctor freed him to eat, and he took the hamburger from me and relished each bite.

On Sunday, on oxygen and holding the podium for support, Dad preached his last sermon three services in a row. I was waiting at his house for him when he got home. He looked pale, weak, and stricken, and he went straight to bed. Though he was 86 at the time, somehow I still thought he would beat the cancer.

On Monday and Tuesday, he did his daily call-in radio program from his house. On Wednesday I woke up crying. I went to a surprise birthday party for a dear coworker and friend, but I couldn't stop tearing up. On the way home I turned on the radio to reassure myself that Dad was okay, but he wasn't on the radio. As soon as I got home, I called his house and talked to his nurse. She told me he wasn't doing well, and my daughter and I rushed over to see him.

Dad was in his room, sitting in a recliner, hooked up to his oxygen and a blood pressure monitor. Although he appeared to be sleeping, he was slipping into a coma. Periodically his nurse would ask him if he was in any pain, if he wanted food, or if he was ready for a visitor. Dad would open his eyes and use all his reserves of strength to shake his head no.

My daughter and I sat on the floor just resting our hands on him. We were silent for the most part, only expressing our love to him in soft voices every now and then. My cousin and his wife came in, and we held hands and stood around my dad. We prayed. Then my cousin, a musician, suggested we sing over him. He began to sing a song, but unfortunately none of the rest of us, not even his wife, knew it.

Looking at me, my cousin asked, "Don't you know this song?"

I said, "No, but I know this one."

I began to sing the Aaronic blessing over my father. He opened his eyes wide and sang with full gusto, leading us all in the ancient blessing of grace. As soon as he sang the last word, his eyes closed, and he seemed to sink deep into the coma. We remained there for a few more hours, but Dad never woke, responded, or spoke after that song. It was dark when we finally left his home.

At three in the morning, the telephone next to my bed rang. It was my brother, explaining that Dad was now in the presence of Jesus. Perhaps it was the way he expressed it to me that made me say, "Praise the Lord." It might have been the assurance that Dad was now in glory. He was freed from the confines of his weakness, machines, and the cancer. He was glorified and in glory. His corruption had put on incorruption, and his mortality had given way to immortality.

It was about a week later when my cousin approached me, saying, "Do you realize we were the last people to hear your dad sing? Steph [his wife] and I talked about it on the way here. What a miracle! Think about it. He sang a blessing over us!"

Then it hit me. I had wanted a blessing from my dad, but I chose to sing a blessing over him. Yes, Dad took over the song, just like he took over my wedding plans, but he gave the greater blessing.

God's grace is the greatest blessing we can give to anyone.

Learn from Grace

In Titus 2:11-12, Paul states, "The grace of God that brings salvation has appeared to all men, teaching us that, denying ungodliness and worldly lusts, we should live soberly, righteously, and godly in the present age." In a previous chapter we talked about how grace produces the perfect atmosphere for learning. Here we learn grace is not only the perfect atmosphere but also a teacher. Grace, contrary to some people, doesn't teach liberty to sin, but sobriety, righteousness, and godliness for the present times.

That's right. Grace teaches us how to live godly lives. Morality is unable to reach into our hearts and teach us this godly behavior. Nor can the law truly teach us or amend our behavior. Both morality and the law are limited because they're external and can do nothing for the heart. But grace penetrates our skin, enters the heart, and instructs us in the way of true godliness.

Imparting Grace

When I was in college, I went on a date with a young man who was studying to be a youth pastor. It seemed as though every other word from his mouth was an expletive. It was so jarring and embarrassing that I found myself wanting to bring the date to a quick close. Finally, at dinner I said, "I thought you said you want to be a youth pastor."

"I did," he replied, cheerily.

"So what do you do about the Scripture in Ephesians 4:29 that says, 'Let no corrupt word proceed out of your mouth, but what is good for necessary edification, that it may impart grace to the hearers'?" To say that he was upset with me is an understatement. He began to justify himself and accuse me of being judgmental. I often think, *If only he could have heard himself.* I ran into him years later, after he had become a youth pastor, and he apologized and thanked me for challenging him. Obviously, he had learned grace in the meantime!

Our speech is to be gracious. It's not to be corrosive in any measure. Gracious speech does not shame, condemn, or find faults. Gracious speech is not lewd, foul, or jarring. Jesus's gracious words, as mentioned in Luke 4:22, were compassionate, attractive, and authoritative. Grace will affect what we talk about and the vocabulary we invoke when we speak.

That's right. The more we understand God's grace toward us and His gracious character, and the more we receive His grace, the more we'll want to graciously speak about grace!

Gifts by Grace

Grace is how we receive divine gifts from God. In Romans 12:6 Paul writes, "Having then gifts differing according to the grace that is given to us, let us use them." The gifts and talents we possess are the benefits of God's grace toward us. He's given these gifts for the ministry He intends for us. They are from the surplus of the sufficiency of His grace.

When we realize our gifts are by His grace, it forces jealousy and envy out of our hearts. When we think the gifts and talents we have are ours by merit, however, we become exclusive, competitive, and envious:

Exclusive—because we don't want anyone to have the gift but us, or we want to companion only with those who have the same gift.

Competitive—because we measure our gifting against others' gifting.

Envious—because we think others' talents are better than ours.

Without grace we can't fully enjoy the wondrous gifts God has given to all His saints.

Too many of us are trying to be what my oldest son used to call "all that." I'll never forget the first time he used that phrase. He was talking about some kid at school who was acting superior to everyone else. "You know, Mom. He thought he was all that." I got the picture when he explained how the boy challenged the other boys, put them down, and laughed at them. Yep. That kid thought he was "all that."

Grace allows us to appreciate a gift God has given to someone else without feeling threatened that we lack that one gift. We can enjoy a beautiful voice even if we're tone deaf. We can enjoy an author's work even if we can't write. Grace takes the threat away and frees us to look for, appreciate, and commend the divine gifts from God we see in others.

Grace also allows us to use our gifts without intimidation or conceit. Peter wrote, "As each one has received a gift, minister it to one another, as good stewards of the manifold grace of God" (1 Peter 4:10). God's grace is manifested in our lives through a variety of talents, strengths, and abilities. God's grace is manifold. As good stewards, or guardians, of what He's given to us, we use these gifts.

I have the blessing of serving with a variety of women at my church. I marvel at their different talents and how God brings us all together, using our various gifts to minister to the women in our body. I've come to realize God never puts all the gifts in one package. He gives different varieties of grace to each of His children so that only together can we fully display the beauty of His manifold grace.

Serving with Grace

This brings us to the subject of serving with grace. Grace is the power, wisdom, and strength by which we serve God acceptably with the gifts He's given us. Hebrews 12:28 states, "Since we are receiving a kingdom which cannot be shaken, let us have grace, by which we may serve God acceptably with reverence and godly fear." When we serve God with grace, we have the right attitude. We're reverent without being self-righteous. We have godly fear without being fearful and condemned. We're drawing from grace the attitude, energy, and motivation for service to God. We serve because of the grace God has shown to us. We serve with the grace God has given to us. We serve so we can show God's grace to others. In so doing, grace naturally excludes complaining, quitting, and resentment.

Resting in Grace

Peter exhorted believers to "gird up the loins of your mind, be sober, and rest your hope fully upon the grace that is to be brought to you at the revelation of Jesus Christ" (1 Peter 1:13). We are to rest in the grace of Jesus Christ. This is where we find our solace. Jesus will give us what we need. Jesus will take care of it. Our hope is to be fully invested in His grace.

Grace is the hope or certainty of our salvation. God's grace is our constant hope or surety that, even in our present circumstances, "all things work together for good to those who love God, to those who are called according to His purpose" (Romans 8:28). Grace provides the hope for the answer to our prayers for those we love.

Commending to Grace

Leaving those we love is always difficult. I hate having to say "good-bye" to my grandchildren. I often worry about them as they attend public school. I pray for them every day, but more than that, I commend each of them to the grace of God.

As a traveling evangelist, Paul had to leave the churches he established to take the gospel to different cities. Often after he left a church, they would suffer persecution or be inundated by false teachers with false doctrine, but Paul was limited in his ability to protect the various fellowships. In those days, as you well know, no telephones existed, mail delivery was slow, and travel was difficult. So what did Paul do? He commended the churches to the grace of God: "From there they sailed to Antioch, where they had been commended to the grace of God for the work which they had completed" (Acts 14:26).

Paul was confident grace would be able to keep them: "So now, brethren, I commend you to God and to the word of His grace, which is able to build you up and give you an inheritance among all those who are sanctified" (Acts 20:32). God's grace would finish the work Paul started, build them up in the apostle's absence, and secure their place with all the believers.

We're commending others to the powerful force of grace when we pray grace over them, bless them with grace, speak to them in grace, and minister to them by the gift of grace we've received. Grace can go beyond our limitations and do what we humanly are unable to do.

Do you ever feel limited in your ability to help others? Do you feel overly responsible for the welfare of others? Then you need to begin to commend others to God's great grace.

God's Great Grace

It's time to draw from the resources of God's grace, to begin to use these resources, and to become so proficient in them that they're our first response to every situation. Use God's grace when you need:

endurance	wisdom	power
patience	hope	joy
love	peace	encouragement
energy	instruction	forgiveness
strength	help	to forgive others

God never intended for us to live graceless lives, merely surviving and trying to please Him with our meager reserves of talents, resources, and strength. Not only are our reserves low, but they're inadequate for spiritual service and lack the divine nature of God.

It's time to begin to use the great surpluses of grace God has made available to you through Jesus Christ. The more you use the grace God has supplied to you, the more grace God will reveal to you—until you're overflowing with grace!

....

Dear Lord, I have often come to the end of my reserves of patience, love, and endurance. I didn't understand that You allowed me to run out of those reserves so I could receive more from Your divine supply of grace. I blamed myself. I asked You to remove my weaknesses and give me what I didn't have. You offered me grace, but I didn't understand its wealth and power. I ask now that You show me how and where to implement Your divine grace in my life. Let all that I do be done by the power of Your grace working through me so You will receive all the glory You so richly deserve. In Jesus's name, amen.

For consideration:

1. List any items, characteristics, people, or things you've asked God to remove from your life.

2. In what area(s) of your life do you need to start employing grace?

3. Review the following Scriptures and share your insights about applying God's grace:

   • 2 Corinthians 12:9

   • Numbers 6:24-27

   • 2 Peter 3:18

- Titus 2:11-12
- Ephesians 4:29
- 1 Peter 4:10
- 1 Peter 1:13
- Acts 20:32

4. In what areas of your life do you need to begin to draw from the grace of God?

5. List some ways you can begin to implement the power of grace in your life.

6. Do you need to commend to grace a person or situation?

Ten

Land Mines

You therefore, my son, be strong in the grace that is in Christ Jesus.

2 TIMOTHY 2:1

On September 20, 1945, the USS *Missouri* sailed into Tokyo Harbor to receive and accept the formal surrender of the Imperial Japanese Army. The USS *Missouri* was not, however, the first ship to enter the harbor. The USS *Revenge* was commissioned to first sweep the harbor of all naval mines placed there to ensure the safety and success of the mission of world peace. A dear friend of my husband's and mine, Will Templeton, was on that ship.

During the years of 1918–1939, land mines were developed and began to be used by military strategists. The average land mine costs less than three dollars, but naval mines cost thousands of dollars. Naval mines have caused damage to ships, submarines, and navy vessels, but they've also been responsible for maiming and killing 15,000 to 20,000 people annually.[1]

Presently, over 110 million undetonated land mines are hiding in multiple locations around the world, ready to cause grievous damage to the unwitting victim who happens to step on one.

Spiritually, undetonated land mines have been strategically planted to thwart, maim, and kill our progress in grace. To avoid them, we must be fully armed and supplied with grace, know the fields where they are planted, and avoid setting off one of these deadly weapons unwittingly!

Be Strong in Grace

Grace is not only our supply of whatever we need and whatever we lack for victory in life, but also our protection against the forces of life. Grace pulls us through the toughest times and assures us of victory. God promises this grace to us in Isaiah 43:2: "'When you pass through the waters, I will be with you: and through the rivers, they shall not overflow you. When you walk through the fire, you shall not be burned, nor shall the flame scorch you.'" Notice that God did not say that *if* you go through rivers or *if* you go through fires, then he'll be with you and help you. No. He specifically and intentionally said *when*. Life is mined with lethal circumstances. The only means to survive them and be victorious in the process is God's grace.

As I mentioned before, I grew up singing hymns, and I still love them. I love their doctrinal content and the spiritual richness of their lyrics. One of my favorites is "How Firm a Foundation." The third and fourth stanzas of this hymn perfectly capture the power of grace to bring us through the deep rivers and fiery trials of life.

> When through the deep waters I call thee to go,
> The rivers of sorrow shall not overflow;
> For I will be with thee thy troubles to bless,
> And sanctify to thee thy deepest distress.
>
> When through fiery trials thy pathway shall lie,
> My grace, all-sufficient shall be thy supply;

The flame shall not harm thee; I only design
Thy dross to consume and thy gold to refine.

Grace is our supply that brings us through the hard places of life. We not only come through these places; we come through better.

I can attest to this power of grace. Grace has pulled me through the hardest places in life, like rivers I was sure I could not ford. I felt overwhelmed by the current, the depth, and the width. They looked impossible to cross. Yes, we all have those tough circumstances we can't see a way around or through. They're overwhelming, and we think if we try to cross we'll drown.

Four times in the Bible we read about God's people passing through deep waters. In Exodus 14, the people of Israel crossed the Red Sea on dry ground after God parted the waters. He used the waters to deliver Israel from Egypt, reveal His amazing power to His people, and destroy the enemy forces against them.

In Joshua 3, the people of Israel crossed the Jordan River on dry ground. At that time the banks of the river were overflowing, and yet thousands of families needed to cross with their children, livestock, and goods. God told Joshua to have the priests bearing the ark of the covenant step in first. When the soles of the priests' feet touched the waters, the Jordan River pulled back 20 miles north to the city of Adam, where the waters stood in a "heap" (Joshua 3:15-17). All the people were able to enter the promised land that day. Joshua had 12 men, one from each tribe, gather large stones and set up a memorial so the people would remember the miracle God did. This memorial would remind the people how God was in earnest to fulfill His promises to them (Joshua 4:1-8).

When Elijah was finishing his ministry, he came to the shore of the Jordan River accompanied by his successor, Elisha. When they reached the banks of the Jordan, Elijah took the mantle he was wearing and struck the water (2 Kings 2:7-8). Immediately the waters parted, and the prophets walked across on dry land. Soon after, a chariot of fire carried the older prophet to heaven. Leaving that site, the younger prophet was again confronted with the Jordan River. Elisha took the mantle that had fallen from Elijah and struck the water, saying, "'Where is the LORD God of Elijah?'" (2:14). Even as he did this, the river parted, and the newly anointed prophet walked across on dry ground.

In each instance the water served as a means for God to showcase His glory and His earnest desire to bless His people and bring them into everything He promised. Grace transforms the overwhelming, overflowing, and overly treacherous rivers in our lives to pathways to God's purposes, revelations of God's power, and surety of His promises.

What about the flames? In 2017 almost 9000 fires erupted in California, causing billions of dollars in damage. Over 10,000 structures were destroyed, including homes, businesses, barns, and warehouses. Over 1,255,000 acres of land were burned, including orchards, vineyards, and fields for housing livestock. Some of the blazes burned more than 1500 degrees Fahrenheit. Firemen worked tirelessly to protect structures and the citizens of California from the destructive flames.

Fire—arbitrary and absolute—consumes everything in its path. The residents who returned to their burned neighborhoods found nothing to recover. The extreme temperatures left jewelry in mounds of silver and gold, and they melted even the safes made to safeguard these valuables.

Life has places very few people survive. God's grace can not only sustain us through the most life-threatening, destructive, and devastating trials of life, but bring us through without the odor of smoke on us. In other words, no one observing us would ever guess the fiery trials we've faced or the fields with land mines we've crossed.

This is the grace in which you and I need to strengthen ourselves. We need to be strong in the grace that is in Christ Jesus. Jesus has made this grace available to us. We're not only to boldly enter the throne room of grace to receive it, but we're to stockpile it, use it, and ingest it. Grace needs to go deep within us, where it can strengthen us. If not, we'll be terrified by or even blown up by the land mines planted in the fields of life.

A ready supply of grace will keep us prepared and protected from all the forces that obstruct our relationship with God, maim our spiritual lives, and destroy our spirituality. Undetected, undetonated, and unscrupulous land mines are out there, and their effects can be devastating. In this chapter we'll look at the harm seven spiritual land mines inflict, as well as at how grace is the perfect protection against their harm.

Land Mine Number 1: Legalism (Falling from Grace— Galatians 5:4)

The apostle Paul didn't mince words when he wrote to the Galatians. Paul had gone to the region of Galatia with the gospel of grace. Publicly, he invited the young, old, women, men, slaves, and free to receive God's offer of forgiveness, reconciliation, love, life, power, and heaven through Jesus. Many who heard Paul believed the word of God and received Jesus as their Savior. Paul later returned to Galatia, "strengthening all the disciples" there (Acts 18:23).

Paul had shared a tender relationship with these believers. Even while he was presenting the gospel, he was suffering from a severe physical affliction. The Galatians were so sympathetic to him that he believed they would have "plucked out" their own eyes and given them to him if that would have helped (Galatians 4:15). Yet something had abruptly changed the affection they had for Paul. Legalists had infiltrated the church. These men came with purported credentials and a false letter they claimed was written by Paul. These men told the believers in Galatia they needed to learn and submit to the Mosaic Law. They said "grace" wasn't a sufficient basis for a relationship with God. They presented certain works, regulations, rituals, and rules they thought the Galatians needed to follow to truly be spiritual. These infiltrators further claimed they were the only ones who could lead the Galatians into deeper truth and help them be truly spiritual.

The Galatians began to fall to the seduction of these legalists. The effect was devastating. The works of the flesh began to manifest themselves again in the fellowship. The power of grace that produces the fruit of the Spirit gave way to the condemnation of the law, which has no power against sin. Competition followed. The Galatians began to "bite and devour one another" (Galatians 5:15). These hapless believers were attempting to be better Christians by trying to keep the Mosaic Law, and they were failing miserably. The old habits returned, condemnation loomed over them, and Christianity became burdensome!

In trying to live by the law, they had inadvertently left the grace of Jesus. "You have become estranged from Christ, you who attempt to be justified by the law; you have fallen from grace," Paul told them (Galatians 5:4). Their attachment to the law had separated them from Jesus. Paul pointed out to them that if the law was able to justify men, then Christ died in vain (Galatians 2:21).

The truth is the law cannot justify anyone. The law is the law, simply a rigid standard of righteousness. Worse yet, no one can live up to the standards of the law, so trying to removes you from the power of grace. Jesus became a man so He could live the righteous life we couldn't live and to die the death we all deserve so He could bring the grace of salvation to all mankind!

One of legalism's worst injuries is to cause those who step into it to fall from grace. It is the land mine all believers must beware. It can also be understood as the land mine of self-justification by any means other than grace! Only Jesus merits God's favor, so only as we receive the righteousness of Jesus do we come into God's favor (see land mine number three).

In John 6:28 Jesus was asked, "'What shall we do, that we may work the works of God?'" In Jesus's time the Jews were used to rigid instructions and "works" they had to do to attempt to court the favor of God. In effect, they were asking Jesus, "What does God want us to do, so that we can be right with Him?" Jesus's word to them was startling, powerful, and gracious. "'This is the work of God, that you believe in Him whom He sent'" (verse 29). Here, for all of us, is the work God requires and wants from us—to simply believe in Jesus, His Son. Everything else we need to be right with God follows from first believing in Jesus. This is the grace of God.

Dear friends, don't let anyone tell you spiritual depth comes by following any methodology, tradition, or restriction. These can cause us to fall from grace. They might look inviting and promising, but in the end, they contain what can wreak devastation and harm us.

It's not wrong to follow a certain way of reading your Bible, praying, or fellowshipping. When you adopt a formula or ritual, however, you can move from the main objective. We read the Bible to grow in the knowledge of our Savior. Reading it to merit God's favor, or to try to be more spiritual than others, will not enrich our lives spiritually. The objective of all Bible reading is to learn about, remind ourselves of, and to meditate on the person of Jesus Christ.

Some people want to tell you "how" you should read the Bible.

They discount the spiritual validity of anyone who doesn't read a certain number of chapters a day, journal, or answer prescribed questions each time they read. Years ago I was introduced to a Bible reading method that employed all three. It kind of swept through our little church, presented as the "right way," "best way," and the "only valid way" to read God's Word. Those who used this method claimed they received greater spiritual insights than those who did not.

Well, I wanted to be spiritual. I love Jesus, and I wanted to please Him. I picked up a one-year Bible, began to journal, and asked myself all the assigned questions. I'll be honest with you—Bible reading became a drudgery. All the fellowship I'd been enjoying with Jesus through my devotional time with Him dried up. Now I was reading to get all the chapters in. I was writing and answering questions, but I wasn't simply meditating and lingering anymore. Subtly, my objective had changed. I was reading to be spiritual rather than reading to spend time with Jesus. The demands were impossible to keep up. Some days required reading ten chapters, and that's a lot of reading for a working mother, which I was at the time. Inevitably I fell behind and tried to catch up to keep the continuity. I began to feel spiritually brittle, frustrated, and condemned.

It all came to a head one day as I was chatting with my mom on the phone. She always had this marvelous intuition, and she could read me like a book. She sensed something in my voice and asked, "What's wrong?"

"Oh," I answered, deeply discouraged, "I've been trying that method of Bible study everyone's talking about. I've been doing it three months now, and I'm just not feeling it. I feel so worthless and condemned. I'm not getting anything out of it."

Her response wasn't at all what I expected. A loud shout of "Hallelujah!" resounded from the other end of the line. "Mom, did you just shout 'Hallelujah'?" I asked.

"Yes, I did! Cheryl, I've been trying to study that way, and I've been feeling so dry and condemned. I couldn't put my finger on it, and the Lord just revealed it to me! That's a great method for some people, but, honey, it's not for us. Let's go back to the way it was when we were enjoying our devotional time with Jesus."

Oh, what a land mine my mother and I were saved from that day! Without realizing it, I was falling from grace. I was trying to justify my spirituality by the way I studied my Bible.

Methodologies extend beyond how we read our Bibles. Some want to relegate how we read, pray, fellowship, and live our lives.

My husband and I were sharing with a young man about how we love to walk on the beach and pray as a couple. He sought to "qualify" our prayer time. "Yes, but do you ever 'pray through the temple,' with your eyes closed and feeling the sand under your feet?"

"Oh, is that the most spiritual way to do it?" I responded. He looked a bit taken aback. "I'm afraid we don't do any of those things," I told him. "We simply burst into the throne room of grace and talk to God directly!"

Perhaps, without knowing it, you've succumbed to legalism, which is related to the land mine of falling from grace. The law doesn't have to be the Mosaic Law; plenty of other laws are out there. Whenever you hear the promise of a greater way, a more spiritual methodology, or a ritual that goes beyond the simplicity of Scripture, beware!

Land Mine Number 2: Exploiting Grace (Using Grace as a License to Sin—Romans 6:1)

The Bible has much to say about those who "presume" on grace as a license to sin. This presumption is lethal. Jude warned about this land mine in his letter to the church: "For certain men have crept in unnoticed, who long ago were marked out for this condemnation, ungodly men, who turn the grace of our God into lewdness and deny the only Lord God and our Lord Jesus Christ" (Jude 4).

Some people take too great a liberty with sin and attempt to justify it under the banner of grace. Having grown up in the church, I've heard more than one person say, "Well, since God is going to forgive me anyway, I might as well do it." That's presuming on the grace of God, and it's a dangerous excuse. It shows that the person saying it is ignorant of the addictive and binding power of sin. Jesus said, "'Most assuredly, I say to you, whoever commits sin is a slave of sin'" (John 8:34). Paul echoes this warning in Romans 6:16: "Do you not know that to whom you present yourselves slaves to obey, you are that one's slaves whom you obey, whether of sin leading to death, or of obedience to righteousness?"

Those who presume on grace think they can sin once with impunity. Like the people who think they can eat only one in Lay's Potato Chips commercials, they think they'll commit only one sin. But then they can't resist sin after they indulge themselves. They fail to consider the "wages" sin charges, the captivating power of sin, and its corruptive nature. No one intentionally sins without causing great injury to themselves and to others.

Second, those who use grace as an excuse to sin are ignorant about the nature and purpose of grace. They have no idea grace is a divine quality meant to qualify us and empower us for divine service. One of grace's functions is the forgiveness of sins, but that's to qualify and empower those who want to fully please the Lord.

Third, they underestimate the glory of grace. They consider it a common thing. They use it like a rag to clean up messes, rather than the royal robe of our calling in Christ.

Using grace as an excuse to sin will result in someone being captured by the Enemy and held by his forces: "While they promise them liberty, they themselves are slaves of corruption; for by whom a person is overcome, by him also he is brought into bondage" (2 Peter 2:19).

Land Mine Number 3: Striving for Merit (Romans 11:6)

Writing to the Romans Paul said, "Even so then, at this present time there is a remnant according to the election of grace. And if by grace, then it is no longer of works; otherwise grace is no longer grace. But if it is of works, it is no longer grace; otherwise work is no longer work" (Romans 11:5-6).

When we try to merit—earn God's favor—by what we do for God, we are no longer operating in grace or by grace. Striving for merit is the land mine that simply disintegrates grace. It's an either/or proposition. We can either try to merit God's favor, which is to attempt to win it by achievement, self-effort, and what we've done, or we can receive it by grace. We can't do both.

I know people who try to point to their past achievements, the success of their ministry, or their present activity as proof they're spiritual. Yet many godless people have done greater works, enjoyed better success, and are actively giving and volunteering in different charities. Their works are more in number and self-sacrifice than that of many Christians.

Do you remember the story of the rich young ruler? By society's standards, this young man had everything. He was not only rich and young, but he had earned a high position. He was in earnest. He was moral. He was upright. He came running to Jesus, knelt before Him, and asked, "'What shall I do that I may inherit eternal life?'" (Mark 10:17). Think about it. To the religious leaders in Jesus's time, this man already had merited eternal life by his accomplishments and good works.

Jesus said to him, "'You know the commandments'" (verse 19). Indeed, the young man knew the commandments and had kept them since his youth. Yet he recognized that something was still lacking. He knew he hadn't merited the eternal life he sought.

Jesus then said to him, "'One thing you lack: Go your way, sell whatever you have and give to the poor, and you will have treasure in heaven; and come, take up the cross, and follow Me'" (verse 21).

All the young man's past accomplishments, all his successes, all his morality could not merit the spiritual life he was missing. The answer was to sell everything he had achieved, gained, and merited, and then simply come back and follow Jesus. This is the way of grace.

Grace, by its nature, cannot be achieved. It can only be received. No one can legitimately point to any past accomplishment, successful ministry, or present charitable deed as validation of their right relationship to Jesus. People who are truly right with God will recognize that everything they have accomplished, any success, and any present kind act is because of God's grace toward them, in them, and working through them. It's all grace.

Paul, in speaking of his accomplishments, said, "But by the grace of God I am what I am, and His grace toward me was not in vain; but I labored more abundantly than they all, yet not I, but the grace of God which was with me" (1 Corinthians 15:10). Paul didn't take credit for his past accomplishments, his ministry, or his present work. He recognized it all as God's grace in him and with him. Should we do any less?

Beware trying to justify yourself before God with past accomplishments, success, or Christian service. This justification is not only invalid; it removes grace from your life.

Land Mine Number 4: Receiving the Grace of God in Vain (2 Corinthians 6:1)

In 2 Corinthians 6:1, Paul pleaded with the Corinthians "not to receive the grace of God in vain." He then wrote to them about the great benefits he'd received through God's grace working in him. God's grace had commended or qualified him as a minister of Jesus Christ, and he listed the workings of God's grace in him in 2 Corinthians 6:4-10:

> In much patience, in tribulations, in needs, in dis-
> tresses, in stripes, in imprisonments, in tumults, in
> labors, in sleeplessness, in fastings; by purity, by
> knowledge, by longsuffering, by kindness, by the
> Holy Spirit, by sincere love, by the word of truth, by
> the power of God, by the armor of righteousness
> on the right and on the left, by honor and dishonor,
> by evil report and good report; as deceivers, and yet
> true; as unknown, and yet well known; as dying, and
> behold we live; as chastened, and yet not killed; as
> sorrowful, yet always rejoicing; as poor, yet making
> many rich; as having nothing, and yet possessing all
> things.

We aren't meant to attempt service or the Christian life independent of grace. The reservoirs of grace are opened to us, and we can draw as much as we need rather than limit the amount of grace we use. Some people are selective with grace. They use it only in some situations and rely on their own strength in other situations. To do so is to receive the grace of God in vain. God's grace is to be drawn from constantly and in great measure to meet all the demands of life.

Notice that Paul drew on God's grace for patience, purity, knowledge, longsuffering, kindness, honor, the power of the Holy Spirit, and love. He called on grace in tribulations, needs, distresses, stripes (lashings), imprisonments, and tumults. Grace supplied him with the word of truth and the armor of righteousness. It sustained him through honor and dishonor, evil reports and good reports, slander and truth, obscurity and fame. It sustained him with life, joy, and the ability to enrich others though he possessed nothing.

Paul wanted the Corinthians to enjoy the rich benefits of God's grace in all situations.

I know I tend to lean on my own strengths in some areas of my life. I try to do for God rather than accomplish something by God working in me through His grace. In those times I find myself feeling defeated when the thing I attempted, or thought I could do so well, fails. I've learned to recognize those times as when I went rogue. I had the supply of grace but simply didn't use it.

The daughter of a good friend of mine made her mother a beautiful Irish chain quilt. She put quite a bit of labor into this queen-size covering, and the result was gorgeous. The young woman had specifically chosen fabrics she knew her mother would like and colors that would complement her mother's décor. My friend adored the quilt, but much to the daughter's dismay, she immediately packed it in a protective covering and put it in a cupboard for safekeeping.

One day my friend's sister-in-law came for a visit. Later, when she went to clean the room the sister-in-law had used, she found the woman had discovered the beloved quilt and used it. She was heartbroken! The quilt had comforted, warmed, and been enjoyed by someone else. Immediately she washed the quilt and spread it out on her own bed. No longer would she keep that quilt in vain!

It's lethal to draw on God's grace only for some of our circumstances. God's grace is in abundant supply and meant to be used in every circumstance.

Land Mine Number 5: Insulting the Spirit of Grace (Hebrews 10:29)

The author of Hebrews warned against another lethal land mine—to insult the Spirit of grace. The Hebrew believers were in danger of returning to the law, rituals, and traditions of the Old Covenant. These believers were suffering persecution for their reliance on the grace of Jesus Christ. There was pressure from without to capitulate to the Jewish authorities in Jerusalem and go back under the Mosaic Law. The author of Hebrews goes to great lengths to show them the superiority of the grace they received through Jesus. He also warns of the consequences of trying to return to a law-based relationship with God that omits the grace of Jesus. Ultimately, trying to serve God by means of the law is to insult the Spirit of grace (Hebrews 10:26-39).

An insult is worse than a slight or rejection. Insult is a deliberate put-down. It's not just saying, "Grace is not needed"; it's saying, "Grace is unwarranted and worthless." This might seem like an obvious part of this land mine to you, but many in the church deny the value of and need for grace. I think this is because of a misunderstanding about the glory, necessity, and function of grace.

Others are convinced that if people receive grace and live in grace, they will be uncontrollable, unhindered, and unrestrained in their behavior. Some serving in church leadership even discourage grace.

During my freshman year of college, my faith was greatly tested. One challenge was from the professor who taught my New Testament history class. The subject was the story in John 8 about the woman caught in adultery, and he told us it didn't belong in the Bible because it was fabricated. As justification for his hypothesis, he said the Greek used for this story was inconsistent with the other Greek John used in his Gospel. He also stated it didn't appear in most ancient manuscripts.

This rocked my faith. I grew up with the firm conviction that "all Scripture is given by inspiration of God, and is profitable for doctrine, for reproof, for correction, instruction in righteousness"

(2 Timothy 3:16). To start qualifying and disqualifying passages in the Bible was a slippery slope. Obviously, those who originally chose the cannon of Scripture thought it belonged right where it was.

I called my dad and asked him about the validity of John 8, verses 1 through 11. He said a body of evidence supported its validity. He lacked the exact data, but he knew a young man who had co-written apologetic books with Josh McDowell, and he was sure he could supply me with the facts I needed.

Before long I was being paged to my dormitory phone. (Obviously, I'm old and went to college before there was even such a thing as a cell phone!) A cheery voice was on the other end of the line. "Hey, Cheryl. This is Don Stewart. I heard you have some Bible questions for me." Dad had asked Don to give me a call. As he listened intently, I told Don what I'd heard in class.

"Well, Cheryl," he said, "the body of evidence to support the story in John 8 is greater than the criticism against it." He explained that the story was mentioned in some of the early letters of the church fathers dating back to the first century, and that it wouldn't be uncommon for John to wax eloquent when he told a story like this one.

Don listed other evidences, but the one that captured my attention the most was this: It's believed that, rather than being added to the Bible, the story was removed by certain early church leaders. By the first century of Christianity, false teachers were already infiltrating the church and trying to corrupt it. Many of these infiltrators were legalists. These men considered the grace of God too heady and dangerous for the general Christian public, and the story of the adulterous woman was too daring for them. They feared if this story were repeated in Christian circles, it would result in infidelity among the wives, who would justify their unfaithful behavior and presume on the grace and forgiveness of Jesus.

These men didn't understand the purpose, power, and protection of grace. They saw grace as license to sin, and this gracious story about Jesus only fortified that premise in their minds.

Though the passage has been disputed by some theologians as to its authenticity and placement in the Gospel of John, Augustine, an early church father and theologian, wrote about not only what happened, but why: "Some were afraid of the passage, lest it should lead to laxity of morals, and so had erased it from their codices." Ambrose and Jerome, also early church fathers, held the same view. Most Bible scholars authenticate this story, but many place it in the Gospel of Luke because of its exquisite Greek.

As Don spoke, I was taken aback that men would try to remove the grace of God from the Bible!

In many churches today, methodology, ritual, traditions, philosophies, and works have become a substitute for grace. The result is perilous to spiritual understanding, health, and power. To omit grace from God's Word and work is to insult the Spirit of grace!

Land Mine Number 6: Bitterness (Falling Short of the Grace of God—Hebrews 12:14-15)

What does it mean to "fall short of the grace of God"? It means to refuse to extend God's grace to others and therefore not receive the grace of God in and on our lives. The measure we mete out grace to others is the measure of grace we'll receive from God and other believers. Jesus said, "'Give, and it will be given to you: good measure, pressed down, shaken together, and running over will be put into your bosom. For with the same measure that you use, it will be measured back to you'" (Luke 6:38).

I want as much grace as I can possibly hold. To receive grace, I must extend grace. This means I must overlook shortcomings, cover sins with love, and forgive often.

Hebrews 12:15 warns us about the danger of falling short of the grace of God because of a "root of bitterness springing up." This Scripture says we must pursue holiness by "looking carefully lest anyone fall short of the grace of God; lest any root of bitterness springing up cause trouble, and by this many become defiled." How does a root of bitterness spring up? Springing up suggests a sudden outgrowth bursting through the soil. Yet something was going on underground before that little shoot appeared. Beneath the surface a seed was germinating. The seed was being given placement, nourishment, and enough moisture to thrive. Out of the seed came the first sprout that pushed and pressed against the soil until it finally broke through the ground and could be seen.

The seedling of bitterness is buried in the heart usually because of a certain insult, slight, or infraction the recipient refuses to forgive and release. Instead, the seedling is given a place in the soil of the heart. It then receives attention when the recipient keeps thinking about the infraction again and again. Tears of anger and resentment moisten it. Unforgiveness attaches itself as resentment. Resentment becomes a grudge. The grudge turns into bitterness. Bitterness shoots up, breaking through the ground of the heart and making itself apparent by obsessively discussing the subject, with tone inflections and corrosive words.

The fallout of bitterness is falling short of the grace of God. Rather than receiving God's grace to forgive and move forward, the land mine of bitterness's objective is to keep the injured party at a distance from the help grace affords. Bitterness often masquerades as justification. We're drawn to it by a compulsion to nurse our hurts and grievances. Lurking beneath the bitterness the lethal shrapnel contained in this land mine are jealousy, gossip, accusation, condemnation, judgment, and resentment.

One of the deadliest aspects of these grace killers is the collective damage they do. They not only maim the one who is bitter, but they maim those who are nearby. They cause disruption and trouble, and they kill the grace in others too.

It's important to make sure the land you traverse is cleared of the bitterness that can cause you to fall short of God's grace. That will mean a daily inspection. Here are some questions to ask yourself:

Do I have negative reactions in my heart when I hear a certain name mentioned?

Do I feel the need to share my cause against this person with others?

Do I endeavor to win people to my side against this person?

Am I constantly curious about this person's activity?

Do I constantly belittle and look to find fault with this person's accomplishments or actions?

Do I feel the need to talk about this person's past failings?

Do I enjoy hearing about this person's faults?

Do I feel gratified when this person fails?

Do I incessantly repeat the same story about this person to others?

Affirmative answers are signs of grace-killing thoughts and behaviors. To be rid of them, you're going to have to admit bitterness lies beneath the surface. You're not only going to have to do a sweep of your life to find this land mine, but maybe even detonate it by confessing and repenting of your bitterness.

Remember, the amount of grace you give to others is the amount you will receive in return.

We can avoid this land mine by cultivating the grace God gives us, praying for grace, and giving the fruit of God's grace to others. Cultivate grace by remembering the Champion of All Grace and the grace He's given to you. Take the seeds of grace He's given you— the forgiveness of sins, the blessings, the mercies, the kindness, the gentleness, and the freedoms—and plant them as often as you can in as many lives as you can. The more grace you plant, the more grace you will reap.

When I was a teenager, a certain pastor was removed from his pastorate for some petty reasons. To this day, I remember my dad's reaction to the situation. "Well," he said in his usual measured manner, "I always felt he was too harsh in his preaching. There was so little grace. He never planted grace in his congregants, and now they don't have the resources of grace to give back to him."

Pray to be filled with grace. When we show grace to others, we're manifesting the Spirit of grace resident within us.

Remember and meditate on the Champion of Grace. Think about how Jesus saved you, forgave you, continues to forgive you, overlooks your failings, and blesses you despite your shortcomings. This meditation on Jesus will result in greater grace for others.

Land Mine Number 7: Doing it Independently of Grace! (Exodus 33:16)

Here is one of the greatest land mines of all—attempting to ford the rivers or survive the fires of life without God's grace. In my life, I have learned, if I don't have the divine grace to go through it, I need to get out of there.

God supplies the grace and even prepares us with an ample amount of grace for every battle we face. When I don't have the grace, I'm in the wrong battle.

God supplies us with the grace for every battle in life. Whether it's the battle of fear, the battle of survival, financial battles, battles of health, relational battles, legal battles, or confrontational battles, all the grace we need to have to experience God's peace and victory is supplied to us. However, when I don't have this grace, I need to either refortify my supply or retreat from the battle.

More than once I've been in situations where I felt my grace ebbing. One time an unreasonable woman confronted me. She was yelling, accusing, and screaming. I knew if I stayed in her presence I would lose my cool. I prayed for the grace to walk away without saying a word. God gave it to me. I've been on women's boards where I felt unproductive and attendance was difficult. I lacked the grace. God moved on my heart to resign.

Grace is an indicator of whether we're fighting the right battles. If you don't have the grace to ford the river or walk through the fire, then turn around and find your way to the throne room of grace and wait there for further instructions!

When Israel first came to the border of Canaan, Moses sent 12 spies into the promised land. Ten of the spies returned with discouraging news. The land God had promised was fertile, vast, and good, but giants were in the land and fortified cities. The spies greatly discouraged the people because of the forces against them. The other two spies, Joshua and Caleb, were excited about the land they saw and certain that victory was inevitable because of God's promises. They sought to encourage the people.

The congregation of Israel sided with the ten discouraging spies and murmured against Moses, God, and the whole enterprise (Numbers 13).

Moses gave the children of Israel a strong rebuke with an added punishment. Because they had refused to enter the land God promised them, they would die in the wilderness and their children would inherit the good land (Numbers 14:1-38). This didn't sit well with the congregants of Israel. They realized they had made a big mistake, and they organized themselves into an army and tried to enter the promised land anyway. This was an even worse mistake, and Moses had warned them against it. Here is the account from the New Living Translation:

When Moses reported the LORD's words to all the
Israelites, the people were filled with grief. Then they
got up early the next morning and went to the top
of the range of hills. "Let's go," they said. "We realize that we have sinned, but now we are ready to enter
the land the LORD has promised us." But Moses said,
"Why are you now disobeying the LORD's orders to
return to the wilderness? It won't work. Do not go up
into the land now. You will only be crushed by your
enemies because the LORD is not with you. When
you face the Amalekites and Canaanites in battle,
you will be slaughtered. The LORD will abandon you
because you have abandoned the LORD." But the people defiantly pushed ahead toward the hill country,
even though neither Moses nor the Ark of the LORD's
Covenant left the camp. Then the Amalekites and the
Canaanites who lived in those hills came down and
attacked them and chased them back as far as Hor-
mah (Numbers 14:39-45).

The first time the Israelites came to the border of the promised land, the grace of God was with them to defeat the enemies.
After they drew back in disobedience, however, the grace was taken
away. Then presumptuously, they thought they could still defeat the
enemy without the presence of God's grace.

It's always dangerous to presume on God's grace. We need to be
sure we have the presence of God and His grace when we're going
up against hostile forces. When I don't feel the grace, I pray for the
grace to keep my mouth closed, and to get out of the situation and
back to a grace place as soon as possible. I would suggest the same
directives for you when you find yourself lacking in grace.

Avoiding the Land Mines

It's best to recognize the land mines treacherous to grace and the fields they're planted in so you won't step on them. But if you happen to step on or have stepped on one of these lethal explosives, healing grace is waiting for you.

Sometimes the best way to know how lethal these land mines are is to have been injured by them in the past. Those who have been hurt by these land mines are often the best proponents of grace.

Life is full of battles. Paul traveled through many fields laced with deadly explosives. He writes about persevering through five whippings with 39 lashes each, three beatings with rods, and being stoned; being shipwrecked three times, spending a night and a day at sea, and journeying often; facing perils in the water, from robbers, from his own people, from the Gentiles, in the sea, in the wilderness, and by false brethren; weariness, toil, insomnia, hunger, cold, thirst, and other incredible hardships (2 Corinthians 11:24-28).

Yet he not only endured these battles, but was valiant in them by the grace of God. God's grace doesn't exempt us from hardship, but it can lead us valiantly through life. We need to be aware of the land mines strewn in the fields of life that seek to destroy the power and protection of grace. We should avoid them at all costs!

....

Lord, thank You for the great grace You have shown me. Please reveal to me the riches of Your grace so I can plant the seeds of grace everywhere I go and in every life I meet. Keep me from burying land mines that could result in the destruction of grace in the lives of people I know. Keep me from stepping into the fields where these land mines are planted. Forgive me for my lack of grace. Thank You again for the way You rescued me by Your

grace when I wandered into those minefields. You are for-
ever the Champion of Grace! In the gracious name of Jesus,
amen!

For consideration:

1. From your life, describe the river you have crossed or
   the banks you're standing on.

2. Note and explain the positive effects grace has on the
   fires in our lives.

3. Use the following verses to identify and comment on
   how you can avoid these land mines:

   - Galatians 5:4

   - Romans 6:1

   - Romans 11:6

   - 2 Corinthians 6:1

   - Hebrews 10:29

   - Hebrews 12:14-16

   - Numbers 14:41-42

4. What land mines have you encountered?

5. What steps would you suggest to avoid land mines to
   grace?

Eleven

Trophies of Grace

The grace of our Lord was exceedingly abundant, with faith and love which are in Christ Jesus. This is a faithful saying and worthy of all acceptance, that Christ Jesus came into the world to save sinners, of whom I am chief. However, for this reason I obtained mercy, that in me first Jesus Christ might show all longsuffering, as a pattern to those who are going to believe on Him for everlasting life.

1 TIMOTHY 1:14-16

The highest honor conferred on any person serving in the defensive forces of the United States of America is the Medal of Honor. This medal has been given to only 3571 individuals since its inception in 1862, and it's awarded only to those who have shown "conspicuous and intrepidity in battle." The actual medal is made of inexpensive materials, but the honor it confers on an individual is priceless. It's a federal offense to manufacture any facsimile of the Medal of Honor or sell it.

The Medal of Honor is a trophy of honor. It signifies a victory won at a cost. Most of the Medals of Honor are presented posthumously by congress because most of the recipients lost their lives in battle. Their families are given the medal to remember the great courage of their relative. These medals are displayed by and priceless to those who have them in their possession. Every medal has a story of some valiant act, courageous deed, life saved, and victory won.

In the same manner, our Lord Jesus, as the great Champion of Grace, has won many medals of honor. These were won as He battled the forces of evil to rescue one victim after another from the prisons of darkness. Jesus said he, like a stronger man would, goes into a weaker enemy's fortress, overcomes him, spoils his armory, and plunders his goods (Luke 11:21-22). He literally ransoms the prisoners from the Enemy's grasp. Then He displays these acquired individuals as trophies to His grace!

No second-class believers are in the economy of God's grace. Every believer is a testimony to the power of the Champion of Grace. In Mark 5 we're told when the disciples' boat docked where the Gadarenes lived, they were met by a fearsome sight. Charging full force toward Jesus was a naked, crazed, screaming, aggressive, and demon-possessed man. I don't know if you've ever experienced anything like this, but I have on more than one occasion. It's terrifying!

Jesus immediately took command of the situation. He ordered the legion of demons to vacate the man's body, and they literally begged him for mercy and to be allowed to possess a nearby herd of pigs. The Lord consented, and the demons departed from the man. The pigs were immediately possessed and driven madly into the sea.

In the meantime, Jesus restored the man completely. When the villagers came out to see what the commotion had been about, they found the man sitting at the feet of Jesus—clean, dressed, and in his right mind. This great display of power frightened the Gaderenes, and they asked Jesus to leave their vicinity.

The man who'd been set free requested to go with Jesus and follow Him, but Jesus had a different commission for this man. The

Lord told him to "'go home to your friends, and tell them what great things the Lord has done for you, and how He has had compassion on you'" (Mark 5:19).

The man obeyed Jesus, "and he departed and began to proclaim in Decapolis all that Jesus had done for him; and all marveled" (verse 20). Jesus displayed His great workmanship through this man's life. His former condition was well known to the inhabitants of Galilee and Decapolis. He had fiercely ruled the area of the tombs. No one could go near that place. His shrill screams during the night echoed in the Hula Valley. He was vicious and self-destructive. He cut himself with stones and knives. He had been chained many times, but he proved to be too strong for any restraints. The transformation of this madman into an evangelist was astounding! His very life showcased the great power and compassion of Jesus! He was a trophy of grace!

In the discourse that has come to be known as the Sermon on the Mount, Jesus exhorts the crowd gathered to Him to let their good works be seen by men:

> You are the light of the world. A city that is set on a
> hill cannot be hidden. Nor do they light a lamp and
> put it under a basket, but on a lampstand, and it gives
> light to all who are in the house. Let your light so
> shine before men, that they may see your good works
> and glorify your Father in heaven (Matthew 5:14-16).

It is God's good pleasure to display His workmanship. He sets His light on lampstands to give light to everyone. This light showcases the greatness of God's artistry, restoration, and power. He uses lampstands—our very lives as testimonies of His work—to draw those in need of transformation, change, and light to Himself.

This reality hit home to me when I was asked to pray with women who would be sharing at a conference for women at our church. It was an evangelistic conference, and women from various shelters and rehabilitation facilities, as well as young impressionable women, were invited to come hear the testimony of women who had been saved and transformed by God's grace.

The women who were asked to share were scared. Most of them had never spoken publicly about the past conditions of their lives. Many of them were afraid of being labeled less desirable Christians because of the nature of their situations before meeting Jesus. Yet when I walked into the room, I was overcome by the beauty, serenity, and grace I saw and felt. I heard the Lord speak to my heart, *These are My trophies of grace.*

Each of those women and each of those stories was a testimony to the God of All Grace who was able to not only save to the uttermost, but to cleanse completely, restore beautifully, and remove any past stain entirely. No shame was in that room—only a glorious testimony to the great power of God's grace.

I remember talking with a young woman who had rebelled against her godly upbringing during her high school years. Plunging deep into the darkness of the world, she drank to excess, became involved with drugs, hung out with Satanists, stole, and cursed her Christian background. It all came to a halt one night when she found herself completely without funds and abandoned by her friends and family. In desperation and with no place to go, she cried out to God, and He met her. She returned home and confessed everything to her family. They forgave her and helped her get the help she desperately needed.

She turned completely away from her former course of life and pursued the Lord passionately. When her beloved uncle died, however, she suddenly felt totally condemned by the choices she'd made as a young woman. She confessed to me, "I feel like I really let him down. He always loved me so much and believed in me. I think I must have been such a disappointment to him."

Knowing this young woman and her uncle as I did, I was able to explain the reality of the situation to her. "No way!" I said. "I talked to your uncle about you many times. He considered you a personal victory! He saw you as a trophy of God's grace. He used to say Jesus had wrested you from the very grasp of Satan and taken you for His prized possession. He was so proud of you!"

This is the reality of God's great work of grace. He ransoms and rescues the undeserving, the lost, the helpless, and the hopeless, and then He transforms them into His trophies of grace. God sets their lives on lampstands to give light to all those who are undeserving, lost, helpless, and hopeless. He uses their lives to draw others to the redemptive work of His grace!

I Married a Trophy of Grace!

Growing up during the "Jesus People Movement," it wasn't uncommon for me to hear testimonies of the transforming work of grace at every church service. Often my dad would have some mild-mannered or even saintly person stand and share how they met Christ. I found these times riveting. I couldn't believe the person speaking had once been held by such strong chains of darkness or lived such a degraded life. These individuals had been freed from drugs, Satanism, occult practices, profound atheism, gangs, and other venues of darkness. Their lives showed no indication of their former lifestyles. My own testimony seemed banal compared to the stories I heard. I longed for an exciting testimony, but I never wanted to leave the comforts of Jesus to gain one. Instead I married a trophy of grace!

I first met the man who was to become my husband at a home Bible study. He introduced himself and said he'd noticed me the week before. We immediately struck up a conversation about the Lord. I was impressed by his passion for Jesus and his knowledge of God's Word. I assumed he had grown up as a Christian, just like me.

Leaving the home group with friends, I commented that he was exactly the type of guy I wanted to marry. He had all the qualities I had ever wanted. I laughed out loud as I said this, feeling completely secure in my single status. At the time I met him, he was holding the hand of another young woman!

We ran into each other again the next week at church. He went out of his way to explain that the girl whose hand he'd been holding wasn't his girlfriend. He had invited her to the Bible study, and she had assumed it was a date. After his explanation, he asked me if I would like to go out. Of course I did! We did go out, and the rest, so to speak, is history.

Brian was reserved when it came to his past. The longer we dated, the more I realized there had to be something there. I met his mom, Carol, over lunch a few weeks into our relationship. I was surprised by how young she was, and she told me about her conversion to Christ.

Carol married Brian's dad when they were both teenagers, and pain and tragedy seemed to accompany the young couple. She had a precarious pregnancy with Brian and almost miscarried several times before going into early labor. Two years later, after the birth of her second child, a little girl, her mother died of cancer. She had converted to Catholicism to save her marriage and because of a deep hunger for God, but her marriage dissolved after the birth of two more little girls. Carol was forced to work to support herself and her children.

Times were tumultuous. Carol's father remarried a woman who was abusive. Then he suffered a massive heart attack and stroke and was committed to a convalescent home while still in his fifties.

Carol also remarried, but the marriage was difficult, and her husband was unaccustomed to the demands of four young children. Carol continued to attend the Catholic church, her hunger for God only increasing amid the rejection of being a divorced woman.

Sometime after Brian and his sisters had grown up and moved out, Carol was talking to Brian on the telephone. During the conversation she mentioned how hard it was not being able to take communion at church because of her divorce. She felt unloved, unwanted, and rejected. Brian suggested she try going to a different church. Most recently, he had been going to Bible studies at my father's church and had noticed how they accepted everybody (grace). He knew an affiliate church was near her and told her she should go.

She did! There Carol heard the gospel as she had never heard it before—Jesus, God's Son, loved her deeply and wanted to be her personal king. If she would invite Him into her heart, He promised to come in and take residency. One Sunday Carol received Jesus into her heart and life, and she called Brian to tell him about what she had heard, seen, and done. Brian was always recommending Jesus for all his friends and family, she said. He was even attending my dad's church to hear the Bible taught. At that time, however, he felt no inclination to be born again himself.

Leaving lunch that day, I had a myriad of questions for Brian. I was getting pretty serious about this handsome man, and I thought I needed to do some probing before I was in too deep! Besides, every now and again, one of Brian's friends would mention something about Brian's former lifestyle and laugh, and Brian would look disturbed. I wanted to know why. Testimonies had always seemed so exciting to me. I had never considered the pain involved in the darkness.

"So what about these stories I hear. Are they true?" I asked him.

Brian was driving, and he gripped the steering wheel a bit tighter. He was afraid what I was going to hear might jeopardize the relationship being established between us. However, after much coaxing and reassurance from me, he opened up.

During Brian's high school years, he moved to Huntington Beach to live with his dad, and his passion for surfing led him into the surfing community. What followed was a life of drugs, parties, and general debauchery. At the same time, Brian had a penchant for fighting. He was involved in more than one brawl and arrested seven times in one year. His dad capitalized on this penchant and introduced Brian to a professional boxing trainer. The trainer immediately noted the potential in Brian and began training him to be a main-event fighter. He was nicknamed the Baby-Face Assassin.

Though he was the Baby-Face Assassin in the boxing club, to his friends he was known as the "philosopher." Brian was always looking for the deeper meaning to life. Though he had moderate success in many of his endeavors—being in a band, surfing, and boxing—a profound sense of emptiness engulfed him. Nothing satisfied the deep hunger in Brian's heart. He tried relationships and found them wanting. He tried religion and found it empty. He tried drugs and alcohol and found them a destructive waste of money and brain cells. He tried the music world and found it vain. His involvement with boxing, unfulfilling. Surfing, his great passion, was only a temporary distraction from the gnawing emptiness he felt.

At the same time Brian's sense of emptiness was growing, a friend of his experienced a dynamic change. Mark and Brian had gone to high school together, and they shared the same surf community. Mark, though, had at one point traded his surfboard for a guitar and found success as a singer in a teeny-bop band. He was on the cover of teen magazines, featured in trendy L.A. venues, and hounded by scores of young female fans.

In the midst of cutting his first album, however, Mark was suicidal. All the success he'd garnered had left him with a sense of despair. Brian knew Mark's parents had become charismatic Catholics, and he encouraged him to take a break from his career and go talk with his parents in Arizona. Mark did, and he found Jesus in the process.

On the phone, Mark said to Brian, "Hey, have you ever been born again?" Brian responded that he didn't know what people meant by that phrase. Mark explained it meant talking to God in prayer and asking Him to forgive your sins through the work of Jesus Christ, His Son, and take residency in your heart. Brian made up some excuse to take a quick break in the conversation and cradled the phone against his chest. *Lord,* he prayed, *I want to be born again. I believe Jesus Christ died for my sins. I know I'm a sinner and I need Your forgiveness. I want You to live in my heart. I give You my life.*

Brian got back on the phone. "Yeah, I did that," he reported to Mark.

The transformation in Brian's life was immediate and apparent to all his friends and associates. When Brian returned to the club to box, the hatred he'd harnessed to defeat his opponents in the ring was gone. He left the boxing world, never to return.

Brian and Mark began to share Jesus with their friends and peers. Mark's entire band got saved and changed the name and purpose of their band. Mark and Brian became roommates and hosted Bible studies and prayer meetings at their house. It was only about a year after these events that I met Brian.

The Prodigal Trophy

Heath was unpredictable. The youngest of three boys, he grew up with his fists always poised for a fight. For some unknown reason he had the proverbial chip on his shoulder. There was darkness over his countenance and it enshrouded him. He was drawn to trouble and trouble was drawn to Heath. Though he garnered some success during his time in the military, he was also dismissed for his unruly behavior.

He came from a godly home. Both his parents loved Jesus, and they also loved their son. They did everything in their power to bring him into the light, but discipline and other efforts seemed to have no effect. His situation seemed hopeless. He was on a destructive course, and the great concern was that he would take others with him. Yet his mother never gave up. She prayed fervently, and she searched the Bible for promises from God and claimed them over Heath. Rather than condemning her son, or throwing up her hands in hopelessness, she invited people to pray with her for him.

As I was walking in the foyer of a business building one day, I saw a handsome young man whose countenance was bright. It took a moment for it to register that it was Heath. "What happened to you?" I practically shouted with joy. "Heath, you're glowing! You even look different!"

Heath smiled, and the room radiated with light. "I gave my life completely to Jesus," he responded.

Honestly, I don't know if I've ever seen such an outward indication of the inward work of God as I did that day with Heath. I couldn't wait to find his mother and hear her version of the story!

When I found her, there was, as I suspected, a grace story. She and her husband had been praying for years. Never once giving up on their son, they continued to reach out, accept him, and remind him of God's love. Then suddenly one day Heath's senses were enlightened. He felt the downward spiral of the drugs, alcohol, and violence. He wanted out, and he called out to God! He volunteered in prayer to give God everything if God would forgive him, deliver him, and save him from the mess he'd made with his life. The change was immediate. Though temptation did not abate for a time, God's gracious power was resident in Heath to resist the temptation.

Heath has continued to be established in his faith in God. His life is not easy; he still has struggles. But he's learning to apply the grace of God to every area of his life.

A Trophy of God's Power

Linda was raised in a morally upright family. She was the middle of three sisters growing up in Whittier, California. Her father was a great provider and devoted to his family. Her parents had a happy marriage, and Linda's greatest fear as a child was losing either her mother or father. The spiritual life of the family consisted of going to church once every five years on either Christmas or Easter and keeping a Bible displayed in the house. Though Linda believed in God's existence, He seemed remote and impersonal. For the most part she simply didn't think about God.

By the time Linda was in junior high, peer pressure became the greatest factor in her life. Her parents saw dangerous habits developing in their oldest daughters' lives and decided to make a move to Orange County, California. Linda and her sister began attending a new high school. Within weeks they'd found the party crowd. Linda dabbled with alcohol and pot, thinking she could maintain some sort of balance in her life since she wasn't part of the drug crowd that hung out at her school. Those people were into harder drugs and drug dealing. However, Linda's quest to have fun meant ditching school, plummeting grades, and bad associations.

Three years out of high school, Linda hooked up with one of "those boys" from her past, although she had never envisioned herself with him. For one thing, he was a drug dealer. After dating for a short time, they moved in together, and Linda partied with him and his drug-dealing friends. Now the drugs got stronger and more frequent. She began to use cocaine and deal drugs herself to support her habit.

After eight years, the relationship crumbled, and Linda entered the L.A. party scene. A string of other relationships came and went.

At thirtysomething, Linda moved back in with her parents. She knew she needed drastic changes in her life, but she felt powerless to enact them. Linda would summon up all her resolve and determination to quit abusing the substances that were controlling her life, but each attempt failed after two weeks.

Then tragedy began to strike Linda's family. In 1989, her beloved father suffered a massive heart attack and died. Then her oldest sister—divorced with three children—was diagnosed with a viral infection around her heart. Linda thought this was caused by her sister's longtime drug addiction. She warned her to stop the drinking and drugs immediately, but she refused.

Observing her sister's life and reeling from her dad's death, Linda wanted to go to rehab, but her mom insisted Linda could rehabilitate herself. Sitting in her room one night, staring out the window, Linda cried out to God. She asked for the power she couldn't summon in herself to be free from the drugs and alcohol. She asked for the power to change her life.

Two weeks passed, and Linda was still sober. Then three, four, five weeks passed, and Linda knew God had heard her prayer and responded to her with His grace and power. Linda knew she also needed to change her social life. She recognized she needed new friends. Passing my dad's church one day, she resolved to go there.

Her oldest sister called around New Year's Day to say she thought she had the flu. Within hours she was on life support, and the next day she died. Her children came to live with Linda and her mom. Just a few weeks later, Linda made good on her resolve and went to church. A few months passed before she realized she needed to give her life to Jesus. Then when the invitation was extended to receive Jesus one Sunday, Linda responded. Knowing she needed to deepen her faith, she signed up for the new believers' group and quickly became a fixture in the fellowship. She made lots of new friends and felt totally at home.

At first, Linda's mother was uneasy about the drastic changes she saw in her daughter's life. When Linda explained her commitment to Christ and lived it out, however, her mother also surrendered her life to Jesus. Together with Linda's twin nieces, they attended church as a family.

That was over 20 years ago. Linda now serves at the church she once vowed to attend. Her life bears no semblance to the former lifestyle she felt trapped by. Most people simply assume Linda has always been a Christian. Her radiant smile, love for Jesus, passion for missionaries, and desire to travel and encourage Christian ministries around the world testify to the awesome grace of God.

A Trophy of Glory

I'll never forget the day my eldest daughter called me to tell me about Tony. She almost couldn't contain her joy, and I was trying to catch, over the telephone, every word she was saying.

Tony was a friend of my son-in-law, Michael. Their friendship stretched back to when they were both young Christians living in New York City. They met after Tony moved back to New York from Miami Beach, Florida, to live with his friends and brothers in Christ—Erik and Daniel.

Together with Michael, the four Christian men formed an accountability group. Since three of the four guys were in the modeling industry, they recognized the need to be accountable to one another, as well as to encourage one another to go deeper in their Christian faith. They continued to meet until Michael moved overseas to further his modeling career and Erik moved back home to Detroit to attend Bible college, leaving Daniel and Tony in New York.

Daniel was in the music ministry at a church in Times Square, but he was struggling with same-sex attraction and refused to be accountable for his own issues. This caused a rift and conflict between Tony and Daniel. Now Tony had no one to talk to about the challenges he, too, faced with his own same-sex attractions, no one to be accountable to and to challenge him to replace those desires with Jesus. Tony felt abandoned and profoundly lonely.

He moved in with a female friend who was strong in her faith. At the same time some of Tony's other brothers in Christ left to attend Bible college in New Mexico. Tony's rooming situation was temporary, and he was finding all his other options for Christian roommates dwindling.

All his life, Tony had struggled with his sexual desires. He had been warned by his friends to stay in fellowship. He did, then he met someone at church who was struggling just like him, and shortly after that he met another man struggling with same-sex attraction who was attending another church Tony joined. The obvious was inevitable. Soon these men were temporarily sating Tony's desires in a destructive way. Also, these desires and practices were dragging all of them away from godly accountability. The attraction felt irresistible. Tony had a hard time trusting people in the church he was attending. He had no one in the vicinity who would counsel him without judging and condemning him.

Tony gave in. He continued to go to church, but desperate for a relationship and a sense of belonging, he remained in a same-sex relationship for 11 years. During this time, his whole life exploded. He began to gain fortune and fame. He had contacts with Christians, but many of them became liberal in their theology and practice. They encouraged Tony to gratify his sexual desires any way he wanted.

Other Christians reached out to him, but at this juncture in his life, Tony had fully embraced his decision to identify himself as openly gay. He didn't want to stay on the fence and play church any longer. He began his promotional career, mainly in the gay nightlife as an event coordinator. He was successful in many varied endeavors, and he supported and raised funds for many of the LGBTQ organizations.

At the height of his success, however, Tony was profoundly lonely, frustrated, and feeling empty. After many relationships, alcohol abuse, drugs, and partying nightly, Tony decided to start a body cleanse. He resolved to refrain from booze and drugs. Shortly after he decided to tap into spirituality, looking into Daoism, New Age, and popular philosophies espoused by a variety of teachers.

Finally, Tony settled into a sort of conglomeration of philosophical spiritualism. He soon asked two other gay men to join him in teaching enlightenment to fellow searchers once a month. The group began to grow and attracted the LGBTQ and heterosexual communities alike.

Tony enjoyed this new venue because it gave him the opportunity to delve into the power of the universe by studying different philosophers, philosophies, and theories about the origins and purpose of life. As Tony was meditating during one of these study sessions, God arrested his attention. Sitting on the floor of his New York apartment, Tony suddenly heard the unmistakable voice of God say to him, *I am the God of the Universe. I am God! I created the universe and everything in it, and I created you to serve Me. So stop running from Me.*

Tony immediately felt shattered into a million pieces. He began repenting for years and years of sin. He found a Bible, and when he opened it, between the pages he found a handwritten message from Daniel, his former roommate. Four pages later in his Bible was a postcard Michael had sent him from London. Tony prayed, *Oh, God, where are my brothers?*

Days turned into weeks as Tony pored over his Bible. He was excited to share his experience with the other searchers in the group he'd established, and he began by sharing his personal encounter with God and what had happened to him. He also shared the Scriptures from the Bible God led him to. The response from the group was cold and disheartening, but Tony continued to meet with the group. Three weeks later, some of those in the group responded to the message he shared.

In the meantime, Tony sought the Lord for godly men he could be accountable to. On a street in New York, he ran into Daniel. Tony immediately told Daniel he'd returned to the Lord. He then asked Daniel for his forgiveness. Daniel told Tony he had already forgiven him years ago and that he had been praying for him. He also told Tony about a men's fellowship he was attending every Friday with Michael. Tony practically jumped out of his skin. God had answered his prayer! Both Michael and Daniel were living in New York and were eager to embrace their old friend.

On a visit to New York City, Brian and I got to finally meet Tony. To say we were impressed is an understatement. Tony is charismatic. He never meets a stranger. He cares deeply for the welfare of all his friends, coworkers, and the citizens of New York City. He is passionate about God's Word. He doesn't just read it; he knows it, meditates on it, and lives it out. He rarely passes up an opportunity to share about his personal encounter with the God of All Grace—the day Jesus searched for Tony and found him looking in every direction but His.

Tony told me God never brought up his homosexuality. That

was not the real issue. The real issue was God Himself on the throne of Tony's life. Once God was enthroned in his life, and God's Word was Tony's sustenance, the Holy Spirit was able to do His sanctifying work in him.

A Trophy of Beauty

My sister-in-law is one of the most amazing women I've ever known. What is most notable about her—besides her big, beautiful, brilliant blue eyes—is her love. Michele loves Jesus. Michele loves all people. She also loves animals, especially abandoned dogs. To meet Michele, you would assume she was raised as a Christian in a Christian home, but she was raised in the same house my husband was.

One of Michele's most vivid memories is the day her father packed his suitcase and walked out the front door. From that day forward, she found it difficult to express her heartache and feelings with words. Her young mother, saddled with the sole responsibility of four young children under the age of seven, was forced to work long hours each day. Michele rarely saw her. When she did, she often cried, but she was unable to communicate the reason for her tears.

At 13, Michele was shy and had only one close friend, Fran. Like Michele, Fran came from a broken home. Her father wasn't a resident in her household either. Also, like Michele, she was a good girl—she also kept the rules. They hung out together at school and spent the evenings chatting on the phone. During one of those evening conversations, the wild idea of ditching school and going to the beach was suggested. Together they began to plan and plot their great adventure. Fran had a more experienced friend who was willing to accompany the two young adventurers on their first truancy. The plan was made and set.

Two weeks later, when Michele woke up on that ill-fated day, the sun was shining. She had second thoughts about the whole scheme, but she felt intimidated by the experienced young girl. So as planned, she stowed her bathing suit in her belongings and feigned going to school. The three girls met up and caught the bus heading west toward the beach.

They spent the day frolicking in the waves, looking through the shops along Main Street, and drinking in the sun. Coming up out of the surf, they felt a cold chill set in, and the sun was a bit lower in the sky than they'd anticipated. They asked someone the time, and to their dismay learned the hour was later than they'd thought.

They returned to the bus stop only to find they'd missed the last bus home. Wet, cold, and in a panic, they looked for an alternative way back. A lone surfer volunteered to take them halfway, and they accepted. The sky was darkening now, and they were sure they'd be in big trouble with their mothers. The surfer dropped them off at a closed gas station in a location unfamiliar to them. There was no phone or attendant they could ask for help, but the outside door to the women's restroom was unlocked. They resolved to spend the night in the bathroom and decide their course in the morning.

Sometime later in the night, they were startled by the sound of a car pulling into the station. They heard male voices talking loudly. The third girl said she wanted to check it out. Fran and Michele begged her to stay quiet and continue to hide in the restroom. She refused and walked out to greet the strangers. The situation immediately turned dark. The male voices yelled at the girl and demanded if she had any friends. Michele and Fran shook as they heard their friend divulge their hideout. One of the men began to violently kick the bathroom door and shout for the girls to come out. As soon as Fran and Michele emerged from hiding, they were seized and thrown into the back of a van.

A gang of violent young men immediately and repeatedly raped each of the young virgins multiple times. The ordeal seemed to last for hours. Having had their fill for the night, the men drove to an isolated road with farms. They dumped the girls out and warned them not to call the police or they would find them and kill them.

Traumatized, ashamed, humiliated, and shaking from the cold, the girls ran into a field of cornstalks. When they reasoned they couldn't return home, Michele said they could seek refuge at her cousin's house. They got a ride from an old farmer who drove them all the way to her cousin's high school. Michele went to the school office and had them page her cousin. Her cousin must have been shocked to see her 13-year-old Michele alone with her two friends so far from home. She arranged to meet the three young girls by a field near Michele's grandpa's old house. The girls went there and waited, and it wasn't long before the police showed up. They questioned the girls and had them examined by a doctor, and then they put them in juvenile hall until they could be claimed by a responsible guardian.

Michele's stepfather picked her up. Neither of them spoke a word the entire four-hour drive home. Michele's mother was devastated. She had no way of knowing just how traumatizing had been the ordeal her beautiful daughter endured, because Michele couldn't voice her pain, agony, or sorrow. The more she tried, the more frustrated she became.

Michele was sent to a psychologist, but even he and counseling couldn't unlock the pain locked within her soul. As a last resort, Michele was sent to live with her father. This meant she had to change schools, and she found it impossible to make friends. She also couldn't handle the mundane routine of school when she was dying inside. She tried to escape the pain by running away so many times that she was admitted to a psychiatric hospital.

Eventually she was remanded again to the care of her father, but she left and hitchhiked north. She lived with a family to whom she'd lied about her age. They paid her to clean and babysit. Then the urge to run hit Michele again, and this time she fled to the mountains.

In a mountain town, Michele made the acquaintance of kids who were just a bit older than she was, swimming in a local lake and having fun. She hit it off with them, and they inducted her into their company. They lived and worked at a farm, and Michele was given the task of working in a cotton field. It was painstakingly hard work, but Michele liked the feeling of doing something so physical. One member of the group Michele felt especially attracted to was Billy. He was kind and attentive to her, and they became a couple.

At this point the only drugs Michele had ever taken were the ones prescribed by the psychiatric hospital. Alcohol had been her main means of numbing her pain. She came out of the field one day to find her peers acting strangely. She asked where Billy was, and someone pointed toward the bedroom. Michele entered to find him cooking some liquid substance. Around his arm was a tourniquet, and he was about to fill a syringe with what he was cooking.

Michele's mind reeled as she tried to process what she was seeing. Billy apologized in one breath and in the next invited Michele to try heroin. Michele was transfixed. Her mind screamed for her to run, but her legs wouldn't cooperate. She gave in, and heroin became her drug of choice.

From there Michele's life spiraled out of control. She and Billy did whatever was necessary to support their heroin habit. They lied. They stole. They spent every waking hour thinking about how they would get their next fix. Sometime amid the mayhem Michele began to feel sickly. Many in the group had hepatitis, so Michele was encouraged to see a doctor. She did, and she learned she was pregnant.

Resolved to give this baby a better life, Michele and Billy took a hiatus from the heroin. Michele contacted her parents, and they signed a waiver allowing her to marry Billy. A healthy, beautiful boy was born on Christmas Day 1975. Michele was 16 years old.

A few months after the baby's birth, Billy returned to heroin. He became violent and would beat up Michele when he couldn't get drugs or something else set him off. Billy's parents took Michele aside one day and warned her to take the baby and get away from him. They put Michele and her son on a bus back to her parents' house, and then she went to live with her father again.

Michele couldn't stop thinking about Billy. Though she was warned over and over to forget about him and move forward with her life, Michele still hoped she could save him. She worked out all sorts of scenarios in her mind. Each one ended with Billy sober and the two of them good parents to their son. One night Michele decided to enact the scenario she had played to herself over and over. She went to Tulare and found the house where Billy lived. She knocked on the door, and a woman answered. Michele asked to see Billy.

Billy came to the door disheveled—and angry. He screamed and demanded to know why she was there. Michele explained that she wanted to help him get clean so they could work on their marriage and be a family again. Billy snorted. He told her in no uncertain terms that he had moved on and wanted her to leave. He slammed the door hard in her face.

Alone in the dark, cold night, Michele cried. She tried to reason how she'd arrived at this place in her life. Having given her son into the care of family members before she left, Michele decided to run again. She found new companions. Some were good, and some were bad. Still unable to talk about the pain that gnawed within her, Michele tried anything and everything to numb it.

At 18, Michele felt utterly trapped, ashamed, frustrated, oppressed, and hopeless. She found a gun and decided to end her life. She remembers little of the incident until she woke up in a hospital room with her mother sitting beside her.

The news was grim. The bullet had passed all the way through Michele's stomach and exited out her back. Her spine was damaged, and she was paralyzed from the waist down on her right side because the bullet had severed nerves to her right leg.

Her mother, Carol, who by this time had come to Christ, cried and prayed by Michele's bedside. God heard. By a miracle Michele was able to dispense with the colostomy bag after a time. Within a year she was walking with a cane and then a brace she wears to this day.

Though Michele was healing physically, she continued to bear the emotional wounds of her turbulent life. Still unable to share her greatest sorrows and aches with anyone, she continued to run, hide, and seek comfort. She would call her brother, Brian, often. In every conversation he begged her to give her life to Jesus. He promised that whatever was locked up within her, Jesus could heal it.

By this time, Brian was married to me, and we invited Michele to come with us to our church's family camp. None of our friends knew the condition of Michele's life, nor did we fully know it. We didn't need to. To us Michele was the lost lamb who needed her Savior to find her, place her on His shoulders, and bring her into His fold.

Michele felt ashamed and out of place among the throng of believers, but she also felt loved. After the camp, Michele's mom continued to send her Bible messages on cassette tapes, and Michele listened. She became more aware of her sin, but at the same time a great awareness of the grace of God was beginning to dawn on her.

One day Michele finally surrendered to Jesus and accepted His offer of grace. When she did, she was surprised by what took place. Rather than feeling the condemnation she expected, she experienced a divine, cleansing flood that poured throughout her soul. All the emotions, pains, and wounds that had goaded her for years were being washed with the cleansing tide of Jesus's love.

Michele continues to shine like the trophy of grace she is to God. Her life bears no semblance to the trauma she experienced in her youth. Whatever scars she had have been replaced with the beauty of humility, hope, and healing. She is a testimony to the beauty of God's grace.

A Lamb, A Coin, A Son

In Luke 15, Jesus gave three illustrations to highlight His search and rescue mission of grace. In the first illustration He talked about a lost lamb. The shepherd leaves his 99 other sheep to find the one wandering sheep. He doesn't give up in his pursuit until it's found. When it is, it's hoisted onto the shepherd's shoulders and carried back to the fold. The shepherd rejoices over the lost sheep and invites his friends to rejoice with him, "for I have found my sheep which was lost!" (verse 6).

Those listening to Jesus could understand the search for a lost sheep; however, His next statement must have astounded them. He said, "'I say to you that likewise there will be more joy in heaven over one sinner who repents than over ninety-nine just persons who need no repentance'" (verse 7).

Does this bold statement surprise you? Have you ever realized the reaction of heaven to a sinner being found and rescued by Jesus? Heaven erupts with joy over every life Christ rescues. The greater the rescue, the greater the rejoicing and glory ascribed to Jesus Christ! These individuals become living testimonials to the power of Jesus to rescue, heal, and restore.

The next illustration is about a woman with ten coins. She loses one of those coins, and she searches throughout her whole house until she finds it. Then she calls her friends and neighbors to show them the coin she found and ask them to rejoice with her.

Again, Jesus ended this story with the same disclosure concerning heaven: "'Likewise, I say to you, there is joy in the presence of the angels of God over one sinner who repents'" (verse 10).

Finally, Jesus tells one of his longest parables, concerning a father and his two sons. Since the parable of the prodigal son was discussed in a previous chapter, I won't go into great detail other than to say this son was a lost cause. His choices had been his own and had led him to a distant land, to a lost inheritance, to lost wages, and almost to loss of life. In the meantime, his father watched the road obsessively, hoping for his lost son's return. One day his hopes were realized when he saw a pitiful figure limping in the distance. Somehow the father recognized the son from afar and went running to him. He was ready to fully forgive every infraction and to restore him to his former position. The father threw a huge party to honor the son's return.

Unfortunately, the story doesn't end there. The prodigal son had an older brother who had remained in his father's house and faithfully served him. He refused join the party for his younger brother. When his father questioned him, he was angry and resentful. His father had never given *him* a party. He brought up all the infractions his prodigal brother had committed. The father explained, "'Son, you are always with me, and all that I have is yours. It was right that we should make merry and be glad, for your brother was dead and is alive again, and was lost and is found'" (verses 31-32).

It's right to rejoice over Jesus's trophies of grace! We rejoice because He has searched out the far reaches of the world and found them. He has hoisted them onto His broad shoulders and carried them to His flock. He has healed them. He has restored them. He calls on us to behold the glory and power of His grace in these trophies of grace. Here is what our God can do!

....

Lord, give me a new perspective as I look at my sisters and brothers. Give me eyes to see them as You see them, as trophies of Your grace. Let me behold through their lives Your passion to search for the lost. Let me behold Your power to rescue the lost from whatever enemy imprisons them. Let me behold Your authority and kindness to forgive their sin. Let me behold Your touch to heal and bind up all their wounds. Let me behold Your glory to bring radiance to their lives. Most of all, help me rejoice, as do Your angels in heaven, over every trophy of grace in Your display. In the name of the great rescuer, Jesus, I pray. Amen.

For consideration:

1. Briefly write the testimony of someone you know who's a trophy of grace.

2. How does the concept of seeing others as trophies of grace affect your perspective of
   - other believers?
   - lost people?
   - prayer?
   - heaven?

3. Read Luke 15 and share your thoughts about
   - the shepherd.
   - the woman.
   - the father.

4. How does a trophy of grace showcase God's

- love?
- power?
- passion?
- desire?
- joy?
- grace?

5. How do you, yourself, qualify as a trophy of grace?

Twelve

Stories of Grace

"This is the word of the LORD to Zerubbabel: 'Not by
might nor by power, but by My Spirit,' says the LORD
of hosts. 'Who are you, O great mountain? Before
Zerubbabel you shall become a plain! And he shall bring
forth the capstone with shouts of 'Grace, grace to it!'"

ZECHARIAH 4:6-7

What a formidable undertaking lay before Zerubbabel. He had returned with the captives of Israel to rebuild the temple of the Lord in Jerusalem, but his task seemed insurmountable for at least seven reasons.

Reason Number 1—The Temple's Utter Destruction

The fierce Babylonian and Chaldean king, Nebuchadnezzar, had razed the city of Jerusalem in 586 BC. In the process he massacred most of the leaders, priests, and soldiers, and he took the other citizens of Jerusalem bound as captives to Babylon. Second Chronicles 36:17-20 records this destruction:

> Therefore He brought against them the king of the
> Chaldeans, who killed their young men with the
> sword in the house of their sanctuary, and had no
> compassion on young man or virgin, on the aged
> or the weak; He gave them all into his hand. And all
> the articles from the house of God, great and small,
> the treasures of the house of the LORD, and the trea-
> sures of the king and of his leaders, all these he took
> to Babylon. Then they burned the house of God,
> broke down the wall of Jerusalem, burned all its pal-
> aces with fire, and destroyed all its precious posses-
> sions. And those who escaped from the sword he
> carried away to Babylon, where they became ser-
> vants to him and his sons until the rule of the king-
> dom of Persia.

Seventy years later Zerubbabel makes the 900-mile journey with 42,392 men and their families across the arid topography to the city of Jerusalem. Imagine for a moment their dismay when they reach their final destination. The Jerusalem they'd envisioned, the city their fathers spoke of so affectionately, was in absolute disarray! The huge boulders that once framed great walls, impressive palaces, homes, and a grand temple lay in heaps of rubbish, huge impedi-ments to restoration. The destruction has been further established by 70 years of neglect. There was little if anything here to work with. Instead these heavy slabs had to be removed to even begin to rebuild.

Reason Number 2—An Inexperienced Crew

The next reason the task was formidable was about the men Zerubbabel had to work with. He didn't have an army of strong men. He didn't have a construction crew at his side. The exiles who came from Babylon were professionals by trade. In the company were priests, singers, perfumers, goldsmiths, and the like. They had lived as captives in the sophisticated city of Babylon. They were used to city life, unaccustomed to the depravations and difficulties of country life. They didn't have the skills, strength, and sagacity to build an edifice, let alone a great temple!

When King Solomon built the first temple, he employed a labor force of over 100,000 men. He selected 70,000 men to bear the burdens, another 80,000 to quarry the stone in the mountains, and 3600 to oversee the actual building of the temple (2 Chronicles 2:2). Not only were many men employed to build God's temple, but a master craftsman named Huram was hired to design and oversee the work of the temple (1 Kings 7:13,40-45).

Zerubbabel didn't have these advantages. He had only the exiles of Israel and a divine edict to rebuild and restore the temple of God.

Reason Number 3—No Building Materials

Zerubbabel not only lacked a construction crew; he lacked building materials. When King Solomon built the first temple, he imported beautiful cedar, cypress, and alum planks expertly cut from Tyre. Solomon also used the gold, silver, and bronze his father had amassed for the temple's construction.

Zerubbabel had only the former stones, damaged and lying in heaps, to work with. The other supplies he needed couldn't be imported. The materials had to be collected by the people who had returned from Babylon. At one point the prophet Haggai told Zerubbabel the Lord said the exiles were to "go up to the mountains and bring wood and build the temple" (Haggai 1:8).

The task was formidable because Zerubbabel didn't have the multitude of resources sent to Solomon. The materials for this temple had to be salvaged and collected from the mountains of Israel.

Reason Number 4—Bad Attitudes

Adding to the difficulty of this endeavor was the attitude of the people Zerubbabel was working with. Not only were they ill equipped for the job, but they were divided in heart. Many were unmotivated, and others were actively discouraging the people.

Jesus said, "'Every kingdom divided against itself is brought to desolation, and every city or house divided against itself will not stand'" (Matthew 12:25). Those who have ever vacationed with a grumpy teenager know how hard it is to get anything done when you're dealing with uncooperative people. Yet that's exactly the attitude of the people Zerubbabel was tasked to work with.

When Zerubbabel established the former location of the temple, cleared away the weighty stones, and laid the foundation, the reaction of the people was mixed. Ezra 3:11-13 records this:

> And they sang responsively, praising and giving thanks to the Lord: "For He is good, for His mercy endures forever toward Israel." Then all the people shouted with a great shout, when they praised the Lord, because the foundation of the house of the Lord was laid. But many of the priests and Levites and heads of the fathers' houses, old men who had seen the first temple, wept with a loud voice when the foundation of this temple was laid before their eyes. Yet many shouted aloud for joy, so that the people could not discern the noise of the shout of joy from the noise of the weeping of the people, for the people shouted with a loud shout, and the sound was heard afar off.

Nothing is more disheartening than to put your whole effort into an arduous undertaking, and then have that accomplishment belittled, criticized, and dismissed! That is exactly what happened to Zerubbabel and his crew. Worse yet, the religious leaders and the heads of the fathers' houses were the most vocal in their complaints. These were the men of influence, but they weren't using their influence in a positive manner to motivate, congratulate, or compliment those working. No! They were a downright deterrent to the nearly impossible feat the Israelites were attempting.

Reason Number 5—Intimidation

Even the wise and wealthy King Solomon felt intimidated by the commission to build a temple for the Lord of Hosts. He wondered how he, a mere man, could build a sanctuary grand enough, glorious enough, and beautiful enough to represent the God of all creation. Solomon expressed his dismay in a letter to the king of Tyre:

> The temple which I build will be great, for our God is greater than all gods. But who is able to build Him a temple, since heaven and the heaven of heavens cannot contain Him? Who am I then, that I should build Him a temple, except to burn sacrifice before Him? (2 Chronicles 2:5-6).

If Solomon, the heir to the dynasty of David, endowed with the divine wisdom of God, and fortified with resources, felt intimidated, how much more intimidated did his impoverished distant relative feel returning from captivity!

Even under the best conditions, how does one build an earthly temple magnificent enough to honor the King of kings and Lord of lords?

Reason Number 6—Lack of Finances

Zerubbabel lacked the finances to build a grand temple. Unlike Solomon, he wasn't the heir to a palace or the bank account of a wealthy father. An exile, Zerubbabel had lived as a prisoner of war since birth. He had not been brought up with counselors, sages, and governors. He had been raised among the other captives of Jerusalem. He was given only a small budget from Cyrus, the king of Persia, when he decreed that the exiles could return to their homeland.

He had no money to hire laborers, import the supplies they needed from other countries, or buy the tools necessary for building.

Reason Number 7—Opposition

Perhaps this seventh reason is the greatest reason of all— enormous opposition to the temple's reconstruction.

Because the land was left abandoned, over the years non-Israelites had settled in smaller compounds around Jerusalem. They established themselves in the land and even obtained favor with the Persian authorities. They felt they had the first claims to the land, and it wasn't in their best interest for the original occupants to be moving back into the territory and reestablishing themselves as a nation by rebuilding the temple and restoring their capital city.

These opponents employed a variety of means to stop the progress. They lied, threatened, showed open hostility, tried to infiltrate, attempted to sabotage, attacked, slandered, and finally used legal force to halt the building of the temple. Their efforts were temporarily successful. The foundation was then deserted for four years until the prophets Haggai and Zechariah received a message from the Lord. Through them, He commanded Zerubbabel to return to the commission of building the temple of God.

Against all these formidable odds, God proclaimed His promise to Zerubbabel through the prophet Zechariah:

> "'Not by might nor by power, but by My
> Spirit…Who are you, O great mountain? Before

Zerubbabel you shall become a plain! And he shall
bring forth the capstone with shouts of, 'Grace, grace
to it!'" (Zechariah 4:6-7).

What God was declaring to Zerubbabel is astounding! He was
telling this weary sojourner the following:

You don't need a construction crew.

You don't need great materials to build the temple.

You need only the presence and anointing of the Spirit of the
Lord of Hosts.

All the obstacles before you will be leveled.

You will build this temple!

When the last stone is placed on the top of the temple, you will
realize it has all been accomplished by grace!

From the time the prophet Zechariah spoke that word to Zerubbabel to the present time, this same promise has ministered to and
inspired many men and women in their service to God. It has delivered scores of people from the pit of discouragement and moti-
vated them to simply obey the word of the Lord. In so doing, many
incredible works have been erected by God's grace!

Perhaps you can relate to Zerubbabel's plight. Perhaps you have
an objective, obligation, or occupation that seems daunting. Like
Zerubbabel, you're facing formidable odds and opposition. If so,
this word is for you. God desires to accomplish the impossible in
your life by the power of His Spirit.

God loves to work against impossible odds. In this way He
reveals His power working in us, with us, and through us. As we
see God's power displayed, our faith is enriched and strengthened.
When we allow God to work in us, we become His venues of grace.

What follows are the testimonies of some of those who have
learned the secret of God's grace and how to harness that grace. In

so doing, the mountains before them have been leveled, and the impossible has become possible. It's my prayer that as you read their stories, you will be inspired to recognize and depend upon the grace of God in your own life.

In Weakness Made Strong

Dawn Vallely is one of my favorite people. I still remember the day I met her years ago. We were both attending a family camp, and observing her, I was sure that her husband, Dwight, had married her as a trophy wife. She had the beauty and bearing of Snow White. Then I spoke with her, and my heart not only melted, but bonded with her heart for life. After we met, Dawn became a leader at the women's Bible study I was teaching at our church in Vista, California.

Like her mother, Dawn was a nurse. The medical profession was so ingrained in her that she even taught classes to nurses who needed to renew their certification.

Dawn had been a nurse for over ten years and was one of the head nurses in the NICU in a hospital in San Diego, California, when she began to feel a strange numbing and tingling sensation on her left side. Concerned, she went to see a doctor. Her worst fears were confirmed when an MRI revealed she had multiple sclerosis. She had been married for only nine months.

She continued to work for another four years, maintaining a full schedule, until one day her speech became slurred as she was teaching. She took a hot shower hoping to ward it off, but it worsened, and she felt weak. Her symptoms only intensified from there, at times paralyzing her left side. Dawn was forced to quit her beloved profession. She became weaker and tripped and fell easily. Even the weather affected her. Soon all her activity and even service to God were curbed.

The doctors tried a series of experimental treatments. She received injections of interferon, but later Dawn learned that because of an allergy to the drug, much of her early suffering had to do with receiving it.

Though Dawn was weak, racked with pain, and fighting depression, she began to draw on the grace of God. She and her husband developed the consistent practice of praying together. Dawn spent time poring over her Bible, reading, studying, and meditating on God's Word. She listened to praise music, prayed for others, asked God for wisdom concerning her diet, and worshiped. As she did, she regained the strength to accomplish the simple tasks of life.

As each day passed, she learned to draw upon the grace of God a little bit more, Dawn began to slowly but surely feel stronger. Naturally gifted as a teacher, she longed to teach the secrets of grace to other women and men who were suffering. She started a blog and wrote about what she'd learned holistically that fought inflammation. She wrote about the great lessons and promises she gleaned from the Lord through her personal time studying her Bible. She answered questions. She encouraged others to pray. She shared her favorite spiritual songs.

Dawn soon began writing and teaching Bible studies to women. Her group increased in size, as did the influence of grace upon their lives.

Most of those living with MS experience some progression in the disease, and just over 50 percent may become severely incapacitated.[1] Twelve years after Dawn's first diagnosis, she's working part-time again in the nursing field she loves. She's also been able to resume teaching recertification classes for nurses. Still, Dawn lives with chronic pain and difficulty. Her disease is not gone. She often suffers from paralyzing attacks. However, she learned in the hardest years of her disease how to draw from and minister the grace of God to others. This is the grace Dawn lives on daily. This is the grace of God Dawn shares with others. She is a living testimony to the grace of God!

A Mother's Grace

My friend Danielle's third child, nicknamed Bubba, was born with a severe heart defect that required five open-heart surgeries from the time he was four months old until he turned eight. His fifth surgery was a heart transplant.

It's emotionally excruciating for any mother to watch her child struggle, suffer, and endure such pain. For over ten years, Danielle felt the intense agony of a mother helpless to spare her son the necessary procedures for the sake of his well-being.

After Bubba's fourth surgery when he was only seven years old, Danielle learned to fully rely on the strength of God's grace. After the surgery, she and her husband, Brian, took turns sleeping in ICU with their son as he was recovering. One night he asked her to play a board game with him, but he became frustrated when he couldn't focus and keep count of his cards. Danielle suggested they put away the game and simply go to sleep. She turned out the lights and rolled her cot close to his bed.

As she was climbing under the covers, her son whispered, "Mom, I'm really scared." Danielle took his hand and prayed. The truth was she was scared too. Her bravado was a shell she wore to comfort her son. It was wearing thin.

An hour later, Danielle awoke with a start. Bubba's bed was shaking violently, and she immediately realized he was having a seizure. She jumped up and called for the nurses. As she waited for the hospital staff to arrive, Danielle inwardly prayed, *Lord, this has been a long ordeal. I can't stand watching Bubba in constant pain. Please take him home to heaven.* It was the first time she had fully released the young boy into God's hands. She was wrung out, as was his whole family. There was nothing else to be done.

The Lord immediately spoke to Danielle in response to her prayer. She heard Him say to her heart, *I will walk you through this*, and a great peace enveloped her. When the doctor and nurses arrived, they were able to stop the four-minute seizure before it could do any further damage. They commended and thanked Danielle for being so calm and cooperative.

Two days later, after extensive testing, the doctors found the reason for Bubba's seizure—blood had been pooling at the base of his brain. The blood had finally dissipated, and he was out of danger from seizures.

Danielle later testified, "Grace came to me in a flood of peace, and He gave me a huge dose of grace that continues to last even to this day. When I have the assurance that God is walking with me, I can be filled with His grace to keep going. I can crawl in the valley or climb the cliffs with Him."

Today Bubba no longer goes by that moniker. He's a healthy young man in his early twenties. He actively serves in our church, and very few of his acquaintances know the miracle of grace he is.

The following two stories have to do with the grace God gave to minister to and sacrifice for difficult people in difficult circumstances.

Ministering Grace

The first hero most young girls discover is their father. I know my father was my greatest earthly hero for years. It seemed as if he could do anything. He loved, protected, cherished, ministered, provided, and even sang to me. I never once had a cause to doubt his love. Sadly, this is not the reality for so many women I know. Their fathers were harsh, critical, neglectful, or completely absent. Yet when pressed, each of them can describe in detail what a good father should be like. It's as if our heavenly Father has ingrained in every heart His own image of fatherhood. To this day, regardless of the type of father they had, I've never met a woman who couldn't list the attributes of a good father.

I never had an issue with ministering to my father. It came easily, simply by responding to and reciprocating the love he lavished on me. But how do you minister to a father who is hateful, unkind, or cruel? My friend Darlene received God's grace to do just that.

When Darlene was ten years old, her father took her and her sister aside to inform them he no longer loved their mother. He had found another woman to love, and he was leaving their household. Darlene's first emotion was relief. Her father was an angry person. He hated the fact that his wife and daughters had become born-again Christians and were attending church regularly. He blamed his own bad behavior and the divorce on the church, their Christianity, and God.

In reality Frank's own vices were responsible for his cold heart. He carried deep-seated resentment against the harsh father he could never please. He hated God because of his younger brother's death at 21 from stomach cancer. He used these factors and others to excuse his drinking, womanizing, and financial irresponsibility. Though he was brilliant and made his way up the ladder in the lucrative software development industry, he was also verbally abusive to his family and terrifying to everyone who knew him.

After leaving Darlene's mother, he married four more times and had numerous live-in girlfriends. On every visit to her father's house, Darlene and her sister were ordered to embrace his current flame with the affection due only to a real mother.

Darlene and her sister hoped for a storybook ending. They prayed for their dad to come to Jesus and for his heart and behavior to change. When that didn't happen, Darlene's heart began to harden. She became untrusting and cold. However, Darlene's mother never stopped showing grace toward the man who had abandoned her. She continued to love him and pray for his salvation, setting an example of grace for both her daughters.

Darlene grew up. One day she was called out of her college classroom and informed her father was in the hospital. Darlene left immediately, and when she arrived she saw a sick, feeble man, isolated and in tremendous pain. He looked so small compared to the man who had terrified Darlene in her childhood.

His foot was infected with gangrene because of his diabetes and an injury with his toenail clippers. For the next several days, the nurses gladly let Darlene take care of him and treat the infected toe. He had been so mean and hostile to them that they wanted to keep as great a distance possible from his hospital room.

Darlene held the bedpan to his face when he was sick. She cleaned around his mouth with a cool cloth. She smiled as best she could and took his soiled clothing home to wash and return the next day. She listened to his constant tirades. He cried often and was suicidal. Because of his diabetes, many of his toes had to be amputated. Other complications arose, and Darlene remained by his side through it all. With every new development, and through all his emotional outbursts, Darlene was given the divine grace to minister to a father who had abandoned her, refused to pay child support, and constantly criticized and belittled her while she was growing up.

She received the grace to let all the unkind words and actions roll off her shoulders. She received the grace to continue to pray for him until the day her broken-down, weary, blind, toeless, and toothless father finally surrendered his life to the Lordship of Jesus. The day he came to know the grace of the Lord, he, too, felt the sustenance of that grace—and did until his death four years later. To this day, Darlene testifies of the amazing grace that overwhelmed her and worked through her to love, care for, and pray for her father. Because of the grace she received and ministered, her father is in heaven today.

Sacrificial Grace

Cindy was sure she would have the storybook marriage. Her husband, Joe, had been the best-looking boy at her school, and she loved him from the day she first saw him. They both came from Christian homes, and both families were supportive of their long-term relationship throughout high school.

Cindy relished being a wife. She threw herself into the daily chores of mothering and homemaking, preparing daily gourmet meals and decorating their home. She constantly looked to her husband for approval ratings. Gorgeous, she kept her figure in perfect proportion, her hair styled, and her makeup flawless. And if Joe criticized her work, she simply added more gusto to her effort.

Then after seven years of marriage Joe asked for a divorce. Cindy was stunned. They had experienced the typical ups and downs of every couple, but she'd never seen any warning signs or indication of a problem that would lead to this. Yet Joe had been having a series of affairs with men. While he'd been lying and deceiving her, he'd also kept up the sham of a nearly perfect husband and Christian.

The grace and provision Cindy received as she prayed for grace were astounding. Cindy was devastated, as were their families and their children. Many of her friends had urged her to give in to bitterness and vengeance, but that wasn't how Cindy felt in her heart. She loved Joe, and she didn't want to see him punished. Somehow, she even empathized with his pain and frustration. Cindy prayed for Joe, setting an example for her children, friends, and extended family to also pray for him. Though they were divorced, Cindy invited Joe over for dinner, and she served every meal with a genuine smile and laughter. Her graciousness tugged on Joe's heartstrings, and he was generous to his family.

This same grace continued to pour out of Cindy as Joe needed reoccurring visits to the hospital. Since his partner refused to take him, Cindy regularly drove him to all his appointments. Cindy continues to minister grace to her ex-husband. He is always present at their family Christmas celebrations. She knows he struggles with sin, but that it's his struggle, not hers. Her struggle was with grace, and she has won her own battle for grace. Now she prays for Joe's emancipation and salvation.

Daily Grace

Many of us have come to depend on the partnership we share with our husbands. But what happens when the personality of the one you love changes? What happens when the one you committed your life to before God becomes like a child and must be tended and watched constantly? From where do you draw the wisdom and strength to cope with the unpredictability of the new person you're dealing with, watch their mental decline, and continue to love and serve? Marsha found hers in the grace of God.

When Marsha and Gaylord married in 1972, neither one of them was a Christian. Then in 1981, because of a work-related injury, Marsha was referred to a Christian psychologist. The psychologist urged Marsha to receive Jesus as her Lord and begin attending church. Marsha started attending my dad's church, where she loved what she was hearing so much that she often checked out his cassette messages from what was then a tape-lending library. Gaylord happened to overhear one of my dad's messages and asked Marsha to borrow a few tapes for him. She did. Gaylord was transfixed by what he heard. After a few weeks he felt compelled to leave his Los

Angeles office and drive down to Costa Mesa to find a pastor who would pray and lead him to Christ.

By the end of 1981, both Marsha and Gaylord were born again, and they both had a voracious appetite for God's Word. Gaylord began to volunteer all his free time from his job as vice president of a major company to serve at the church. Marsha often accompanied him.

When my husband took the pastorate of a small church in Vista, California, Gaylord and Marsha often drove down from Orange County to help us. Gaylord and my dad worked together to remodel the church building, which had been an Elks Lodge. Marsha set up a tape-lending ministry with Brian's cassette messages at our church. After they'd helped us for a year, Brian asked Gaylord if he would consider moving to Vista and becoming the assistant pastor of the growing fellowship. Gaylord and Marsha joined us.

Gaylord was smart and accomplished. He could do just about anything. He could balance bank accounts, oversee finances, make wise decisions, fix broken pipes, remodel, counsel, and even repair appliances. Marsha had been the more unassuming partner in the duo. Once she retired from her job, she loved being taken care of and was unaccustomed to having to do much in the way of work, other than making dinner and keeping the house clean. Marsha's passions were in her crafts, ministry to friends, and sharing her faith.

They lived in Vista until they took a long road trip across the United States in their motorhome. Gaylord was an excellent driver. He could move the cumbersome bus through narrow lanes, in heavy traffic, and on country roads. Marsha felt relaxed with Gaylord at the wheel. They returned to Vista after their long adventure. Then my father asked Gaylord to consider a position at his church in Costa Mesa, California. Gaylord prayed and accepted. The couple moved to Orange County and Gaylord joined the staff.

Gaylord had always had a laidback personality. Nothing seemed to stress him, so when he began to show signs of anxiety, Marsha was concerned. Then he began to decline mentally. His personality began to change as well, and he became confused and disoriented easily. It was difficult for Marsha to cope with these changes at first because the person Gaylord was becoming was so drastically different from the man he'd once been. Soon Gaylord was officially diagnosed with Alzheimer's disease.

Marsha became the sole caregiver for her husband, and she never had a break. The care was constant and high maintenance. People with Alzheimer's are as different in behavior as fingerprints are different, but the commonality they all share is their growing self-involvement, childlikeness, and mounting insecurities.

Marsha continues to take daily care of Gaylord. He's forgotten her name and often calls her "Mom." She tells him how much she loves him every day, and he responds with a nod or tears. Marsha has never told Gaylord his condition is terminal because she doesn't want to darken the years he has left.

One of the most difficult aspects of her new life is the profound loneliness she sometimes feels. At first, she struggled with feelings of bitterness and resentment when people didn't return her phone calls or respond to her emails. Then God gave her the grace to understand the busyness others struggle with and to avoid such high expectations for them. She has allowed the isolation of her life to prove that Jesus is her Friend who is closer than a brother (Proverbs 18:24).

Today Gaylord mainly speaks gibberish. It's difficult for them to get out of the house because his moods are unpredictable. He cries daily, and Marsha endeavors to comfort him with God's Word and promises. She testifies that she would never trade her journey for something more comfortable. Through this time, she has come to know the faithfulness, love, and grace of God in an unfathomable measure. Early in their marriage, after both Gaylord and Marsha had come to Christ, the theme of their lives came from Isaiah 6:8: "I heard the voice of the Lord, saying: 'Whom shall I send, and who will go for Us?' Then I said, 'Here am I! Send me.'" This theme continues to resonate in Marsha's heart when she wakes and contemplates another day of ministering to Gaylord. She looks up and whispers softly to the Lord, "Here am I! Send me."

Extraordinary Grace

I met Kris Repp at a missionary conference in Austria. Kris is tall, elegantly beautiful, and in her fifties. She has long, flowing locks of gray hair she wears pulled back in a ponytail. She has the bearing and grace of a yoga instructor, and I fully expected teaching yoga to be her occupation. I was totally wrong! One afternoon she approached me and asked if we could chat. Kris felt compelled to share her story with me. I am so glad she did.

Kris had gone on various outreaches with her church in Seattle, Washington, before her divorce. As a nurse, she could help minister to those who were sick or injured. When her husband left, however, Kris concentrated on raising their two sons.

Then two years after her separation, Kris was asked to serve in a medical clinic in Mexico. The offer intrigued Kris. She had a deep longing for missionary life and to help people in impoverished countries. Her eldest son was spending a year away from home in a high school exchange program, but her youngest son was still under her care, and she didn't think her estranged husband would agree to his spending a year abroad with his mother as she served in a clinic. Kris almost refused the offer outright, but something moved in her to wait and pray. As Kris prayed, the desire to go increased. She decided to fast and pray and then talk with her husband. Kris was stunned when he readily agreed to release their son to go with her.

Kris called back to say she'd accept the offer, but while she'd been praying, someone else had been chosen to fill the vacancy. She said to the recruiter, "You must have some other place you can send me. I know God wants to send me, or my husband would never have agreed to let my son go."

Kris was invited to go to Roatan, Honduras, to pioneer a new work. Roatan is an island in the Caribbean. On one side are scenic beaches and hotels, and where tourists snorkel in the crystalline waters. The other side is filled with abject poverty and primitive conditions. Kris was going to this other side. She quit her job, packed her bags, and with her son beside her set off to live at and establish a clinic on a tropical island. After arriving, it became obvious that the pioneering plans must be put on hold, but Kris remained in her post for another month, accepting the sweltering heat, mosquitos, barking dogs, and humidity as preparation for whatever mission call would come next.

She was soon invited to Guatemala, Central America, where she had many opportunities to use her nursing skills. Kris's son attended an international school in the city while she worked in a medical clinic in the squatter's camp in the city dump and learned Spanish. Not long after her arrival, she met another missionary who drafted her to translate for the teams with which he worked, taking the gospel to the indigenous mountain villages. Kris accompanied him and was immediately drawn to these mountain people. She remained there to work and minister among these villages for another five years.

Kris's life began to weave back and forth between visits and short stays in Seattle and traveling to set up medical clinics in some of the most remote, dirtiest, impoverished, dangerous, and darkest places on earth.

Despite enduring muggings, arson fires, being placed under arrest in a communist country (but never threatened by terrorists), contracting malaria, deprivation, and countless discomforts, she has continued to serve the Lord for 22 years. She's traveled the globe, sharing the gospel, setting up clinics, setting broken bones, extracting rotten teeth, cleansing wounds, dealing with infections, dispensing medicine, stitching up gaping wounds, bandaging sores, and any other procedure required.

Kris daily relies on the grace of God for her strength, wisdom, courage, direction, and endurance.

I will never forget that first conversation we shared years ago. She mentioned some friends she stayed with when she was on furlough, and that they were wealthy. My jaw dropped. At the time I was having a private struggle with grace. I had developed an anti-materialistic attitude, and I was resentful of what I perceived to be wasteful living in the place I was living. I think I harbored a private sense of guilt because I, myself, was not serving on the mission field. I was living in the comforts of home while my fellow brothers and sisters in Christ were enduring extreme hardships and making great sacrifices.

When Kris mentioned her wealthy acquaintances, I asked how she dealt with reconciling the abject poverty and need she experienced with the comforts and excesses she saw in Seattle. Her look was so gentle and disarming. A tender smile swept across her beautiful face, and she said, "Cheryl, I am a missionary wherever I am. As a missionary, I don't judge my mission field or the people there. I simply seek to minister to them the grace and love of Jesus."

I have never had a poker face, and my facial expression must have betrayed my heart issues, because she asked, "Are you struggling with grace for the mission field in Orange County?"

"Does it show?" I asked.

"Just a little bit," she answered, graciously. Then she asked if she could pray for me. As she prayed, I felt every iota of gracelessness vacate my body. Tears streamed down my cheeks.

Kris has been given an extreme and extraordinary grace to travel, endure, and minister in ways you and I might never experience. Yet wherever she is, no matter what class of people are there, Kris pours out the extreme grace of Jesus to others.

Enabling Grace

Sarah is a vivacious young woman with a personality that immediately draws you in. She loves people, and that love can be felt. Probably the most notable thing about Sarah is that she's the eldest daughter from a family of seven children. She grew up in Southern California and spent most of her youth frolicking in the waves along the beaches in Orange County.

At 16, Sarah was already working at her church in a book distribution ministry. Working with books was the perfect outlet for her. She loved to read, and her favorite books were missionary biographies. She tried to pacify the restlessness in her heart with imagining the far-off places and cultures where her missionary heroes and heroines served.

Sarah excelled in this ministry. She worked well with people, she was intelligent, and she was well organized. She had such great management skills that by the time she was in her early twenties she was supervisor over the entire ministry.

In the meantime, her younger sister, Rachel, who is also her best friend, was working with an American pastor in England named

Phil Pechonis. They were facilitating a Christian musical festival in Southern England called Creation Fest. Sarah delighted in anything her little sister did. She had boundless energy, exuberance, and great ideas. Watching her help organize this big event piqued Sarah's curiosity. She wanted to see the festival where Rachel had invested so much of her time and effort.

Sarah accompanied Rachel and the team from their church to Cornwall, England, in 2009. Rachel immediately put Sarah to work helping organize tents, booths, servers, greeters, and in just about any and every area where she could serve. Sarah loved it. She also met and hit it off with Phil Pechonis, the initiator and overseer of the festival.

Returning home to California, the restlessness in Sarah's heart couldn't be ignored. Talking with Rachel, she realized they both shared the same sense of disquiet and felt God had something for them outside of California, just beyond their reach. Together they planned a year-long trip, traveling across three different continents and visiting the Christian ministries they knew of in each country they chose.

In 2010 Sarah and Rachel took off on their adventure. They loved everywhere they visited and the missionaries they met, as well as the ministries they experienced. Never overstaying their welcome, they proved to be a blessing wherever they stayed.

While traveling, Rachel met the man who would prove to be her soul mate and ministry partner. Sarah knew she wouldn't be losing a sister but gaining a brother. Still, the thought left her a bit more restless. She knew she couldn't return to her old job; she needed someplace new to serve. At the same time, her church was looking for a communications director, and she got the job. In this role Sarah helped the different ministries communicate and coordinate with one another as well as helped plan, organize, and execute events ranging from 500 to 5000 people in attendance. This new job also meant Sarah helped coordinate Creation Fest from stateside.

In the meantime, Creation Fest continued to grow, attracting thousands of people from all over England. The festival included strong Bible teaching, apologetic and biblical workshops, worship, games, a skate park, bouncy castles, kids' programs, and camping.

Sarah again proved to be outstanding at her job. She served as communications director at the church until 2014, when her services were required in England because Phil Pechonis was gravely ill with cancer. Although it seemed like he was rallying, he needed help. Then the morning after Sarah landed in England, she learned Phil was in the presence of Jesus. Sarah was needed to step in and take over.

No one could imagine Creation Fest without Phil. He was one of those amazing individuals who could go anywhere, do practically anything, and make things happen. He had an irresistible faith in God and a passion for the gospel. It was quietly decided that after 2014, Creation Fest would be put to rest, but 2014 turned out to be the greatest year Creation Fest had ever experienced. More people and more kids attended than in any of the previous years. Also, more commitments were made to Jesus than in the previous years. It was as if the festival had finally gained credibility with the community, and it just seemed wrong to stop the festival now. It was obvious that God's anointing was on it.

Someone suggested to Sarah that she might take Phil's position to keep the festival going. The thought was daunting, but the more Sarah tried to push it away, the stronger it grew. Still in England, she found a teashop in Plymouth, where she could be alone and read her Bible. The Lord quickened her attention to Isaiah 49:1-10. As she read, it seemed as if every verse was directing her to the coastlands of England to serve the Lord in the special capacity for which He had created her. Sarah wanted to be sure this was from God. She scribbled a date and short notation in her Bible, and then she decided to hide this idea away in her heart and wait for confirmation.

The confirmation came the next day when a couple she hadn't seen in six years approached her. They asked if they could pray for her. As they did, it was as if they were directly praying Isaiah 49 over her. They couldn't have known these were the very verses with which Sarah felt the Lord prompting her heart.

Sarah tentatively approached my husband, Brian, who was in England as well, and said, "I think maybe I'm supposed to stay here and run Creation Fest." Later she recalled that Brian's face looked blank. She waited for a response, but he just turned and walked away. *Well, that's over*, she thought.

To be honest, the Creation Fest board was looking for a man to oversee the festival, thinking a man would be best for such a huge undertaking. However, no man they knew, British or American, was in a position to step in.

Brian caught up with Sarah the next day. "Would you be willing to stay here and oversee preparations for the next Creation Fest? We'll just plan on doing it next year and see how it goes." That was four years ago. Today Creation Fest is a mainstay event every August at the Cornwall Fairgrounds. It continues to grow yearly in size and fame.

The festival is a huge endeavor with more than 10,000 visitors and more than 2000 campers. The children's program has almost 800 children in attendance. Almost 60,000 people watch the live stream on the internet. As they would say in England, "It's massive!"

Behind all the activity is this vibrant young woman named Sarah. I was able to spend a few minutes with her recently over a cup of coffee. I asked if I could use her story to highlight God's grace. Her life is so amazing to me. She's a single young woman living in a foreign

country. She works at the Creation Fest office in Wadebridge, Cornwall, near the bus station. She's known by most of the people living in the Cornish town. Throughout the year, she and her team
host kids' clubs, sporting outreaches, and prayer meetings. She also
works with local churches and churches all over England to coordinate evangelistic outreaches and prayer meetings. She's a frequently
requested speaker throughout the country and all over the world,
speaking at social clubs, retreats, luncheons, churches, and wherever
else God opens a door for her to share the glorious gospel of Jesus.

I asked Sarah how she maintains the supply of grace she needs
to manage all the activity in her life. She told me her greatest supply of grace comes from her daily devotional time. During that sol-
itary hour she prays, reads her Bible, and then meditates on God's
Word. She also spends time fellowshipping with her two South Afri-
can roommates, who are also her friends and coworkers. She told me
she intentionally seeks out godly people who walk closely with Jesus
and allows these individuals to pour God's grace into her.

To an outsider Sarah's life looks daunting, and it is. This life is
only possible for her when she continually draws upon God's grace.

Grace unto Death

For years I had heard about Ian Squires. He attended a church in
England our friend pastored, and our friend dearly loved him and
often shared with us the work Ian was doing in Africa.

Ian was an optician. He owned his own shop on a bustling corner in Shepperton, Surrey, in the United Kingdom. In his spare
time, he created a portable, solar-powered lens grinder. Since these
machines didn't require electricity, they worked well for the tribes-
men in Nigeria Ian had been ministering to. In 2003 he created his
own Christian charity—Mission for Vision. He raised money, collected old eyeglasses, and used the funds gathered to manufacture

his lens grinders and take them to the impoverished regions of Nigeria. There he set up clinics where he trained men and women to give eye exams, make the lenses, and fit adults and children with glasses.

In 2013 Ian began to work closely with the missionary organization New Foundations. He traveled with them often to a compound in Enekorogha, Nigeria. There he worked in their clinic with doctors and nurses, examining patients from early morning until sundown. Ian would conduct eye exams, make glasses, and fit those he attended with the proper eyewear, all the while training others to take over when he left. He and the four-member team spent their nights in accommodations right next to the clinic.

In early October 2017, Ian left England with the three other members of New Foundations charity and flew to Nigeria to minister once more at the Enekorogha compound. Since the remote village was in South Nigeria, they weren't overly concerned about violence. Also, they had won the respect of the people there because of the help and services they'd provided. Yet in the early morning of October 3, sometime just after midnight, militants rudely awakened the New Foundations team. The gang violently ransacked the compound and collected the team's possessions. Then they grabbed them all and took them hostage.

Ian and the others were taken to an undisclosed location and carefully guarded. The militants were armed and nervous. Ian tried to keep the spirits of the other three hostages hopeful. They played the game The Unbelievable Truth, where you try to discern fact from fiction. While they played, one of the militants brought them a guitar they'd taken with the violent intrusion. Ian picked up the guitar and began to play and sing the hymn "Amazing Grace." The other three joined in, and as they sang they felt their spirits lift. Ian had just finished the last stanza when suddenly a round of bullets rifled through his body. He died instantly. The other three dived for cover in the jungle and only returned when the militants brought them back. Ian's assailant was never identified. A few days later a settlement was negotiated between the government and the militants, and the other team members were released.

Amid the most harrowing circumstances imaginable, Ian Squires chose to sing about the grace of God. It was the reminder and contemplation of this grace that raised the spirits of his fellow captives. Ian Squires entered the gates of heaven with a song of God's grace on his lips.

You Have a Grace Story

You have a grace story. It's yet to be recorded, but it's in you. You need only to look back across the years of your life to recognize the grace of God toward you. I remember asking a 90-year-old man I knew when he'd been saved. He shook his finger at me and said, "Oh no. We can't start there. Even though I finally surrendered when I was in my forties, I trace the grace of God in my life all the way back to my childhood." He then started with the gracious providence of God that had begun even before he was born to direct the events of his life.

The same is true for you. God's grace toward you began even before you were born, or conceived. He has been exercising His grace toward you in a myriad of ways. By His grace you live. By His grace you are saved. By His grace you are sustained. By His grace you are strengthened. By His grace you are enabled. By His grace you are sanctified. By His grace God works His character, goodness, and gifts into your life.

I don't know what the circumstances of your life are, but I know God's grace is more than you ever expected. I know God's grace is all you'll ever need for whatever life throws at you. As you begin to explore and embrace the grace of God for you, your own story of grace will be realized.

God's grace is waiting for you. God's grace is more than you ever expected and all that you will ever need!

....

Dear Father God, thank You for the grace You have so richly provided. Help me continue to search out this great grace. Show me again and again how to appropriate this grace into my life. Fill me with Your grace that I might overflow with grace. Let others see Your grace in me. Use my life to write a grace story that will attract others to You. Help me to bless others with the grace You have so richly poured out on me. In the gracious name of Jesus, amen.

For consideration:

1. Take a moment to trace God's grace in your own life. Where did it begin?

2. In what area of your life has God's grace been the most evident?

3. If you were to write your own grace story, what would you title it?

4. Read Zechariah 4:6-10 and answer the following questions:

   - What obstacles or opposition are you presently facing?

   - What inspiration do you receive from the fact that God promised that Zerubbabel would finish the temple?

- What does it mean to you to know that God rejoices over even the small things in our lives?
- How does the fact that the words "Grace, grace to it!" would be shouted when the capstone of the temple was brought forth minister to you?
- How can you apply Zechariah 4:6 to your life today?

5. Why is God's grace beyond your expectations?

6. How is God's grace all we need? (See also 2 Corinthians 9:8 and 12:9.)

Acknowledgments

When it comes to grace, the first and foremost to be acknowledged is the Lord Jesus Christ, who graciously gave His life for me that I might be saved, empowered, and blessed through His magnificent grace. I am thankful for the grace He lavished on me in giving me my gracious parents, Chuck and Kay Smith, who were the first to introduce and exemplify God's grace to me. I am also so very grateful for God's gift to me in my wonderful husband who has ceaselessly delighted me with his gracious kindness, love, forgiveness, and humor through 38 years of marriage. In God's wisdom He also gave me Kristyn, Char, Kelsey, and Braden. These four dynamic offspring were relentless in their quest to bring their mother into the full acknowledgment and dependency on God's grace. I don't think I could have truly understood the riches of God's grace without them! Then there are my precious friends who prayed, submitted their stories, helped me with edits, and believed in this book. Their constant encouragement was a catalyst to go deeper into the riches of God's grace. My thankfulness continues to extend to Harvest House and especially Bob Hawkins for his enthusiasm and urgings to write this book, and for pairing me with the brilliant and gracious Kathleen Kerr. Her encouragements made my heart soar. Also, I was overjoyed with the edits of Betty Fletcher and Jean Bloom. They truly put the Z in zing.

Notes

Chapter Two—What's So Great About Grace?

1. Michael E. Ruane, "How Julia Ward Howe Wrote 'The Battle Hymn of the Republic'—Despite Her Husband," *The Washington Post*, November 18, 2011.

Chapter Three—The Battle

1. Enjoli Perfume "Because I'm a Woman" commercial, https://www.youtube.com/watch?v=_Q0P94wyBYk

Chapter Four—The Enemies of Grace

1. Jill Canon, *Civil War Heroines* (Santa Barbara, CA: Bellerophon Books, 1995), 52.

Chapter Five—Qualified by Grace

1. National Institute of Justice, "Recidivism," https://www.nij.gov/topics/corrections/recidivism/Pages/welcome.aspx

2. Jonathan Aitken, *John Newton: From Disgrace to Amazing Grace* (Wheaton, IL: Crossway, 2007).

Chapter Six—The Armory of Grace

1. For background and further details of the story of Hubert Mitchell and his family, read his niece Arlita Morken Winston's book *Heart-Cry* (Victoria, BC, Trafford Publishing), 145-49. Arlita and her parents, David and Helen Morken, were also missionaries with Hubert and Helen Mitchell in the jungles of Sumatra.

2. Learn more at www.homemakerscorner.com/ajf-annie.htm.

Chapter Eight—Enlisted in Grace

1. Hudson Taylor, *China* (London: James Nisbet and Company, 1865), 14.

Chapter Nine—Use It or Lose It

1. Christine Hunter, *The Little Woman* (Chicago, IL: Moody Publishing, 1970).

Chapter Ten—Land Mines

1. Unicef, "Children and Landmines," https://www.unicef.org/french/protection/files/Landmines_Factsheet_04_LTR_HD.pdf

Chapter Twelve—Stories of Grace

1. Healthline, "Multiple Sclerosis by the Numbers, https://www.healthline.com/health/multiple-sclerosis/facts-statistics-infographic

About the Author

Cheryl Brodersen, the daughter of Pastor Chuck and Kay Smith, is a popular speaker and the author of *When a Woman Lets Go of the Lies* and *When a Woman Lets Go of Her Fears,* and coauthor with her husband of *Growing Together as a Couple.* She also hosts *Living Grace* on CalvaryChapel.com and is a radio cohost every Friday afternoon on Pastor's Perspective with her husband, Pastor Brian Brodersen. Currently Cheryl and Brian serve at Calvary Chapel Costa Mesa in California.

Other Books by Cheryl Brodersen

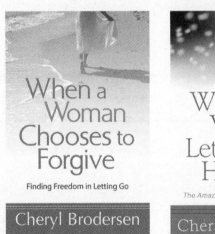

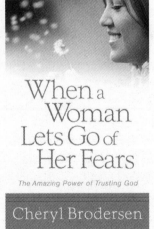

To learn more about Harvest House books and
to read sample chapters, visit our website:

www.harvesthousepublishers.com